T0319651

AN AGE OF RISK

AN AGE OF RISK

POLITICS AND ECONOMY IN

EARLY MODERN BRITAIN

EMILY C. NACOL

Princeton University Press
Princeton & Oxford

Published by Princeton University Press,
41 William Street, Princeton, New Jersey 08540
In the United Kingdom: Princeton University Press,
6 Oxford Street, Woodstock, Oxfordshire OX20 1TR
press.princeton.edu

ISBN 978-0-691-16510-3

Library of Congress Control Number 2016942224

British Library Cataloging-in-Publication Data is available

This book has been composed in ITC New Baskerville Std

Printed on acid-free paper ∞

Printed in the United States of America

1 3 5 7 9 10 8 6 4 2

For my parents

CONTENTS

ACKNOWLEDGMENTS

Although writing a book can often feel like a very solitary enterprise, acknowledgment pages tell the true story—that authors are supported by communities. I am very fortunate and happy to thank my community here, by naming the institutions and people who have helped me with *An Age of Risk*.

I would be remiss not to start by thanking the people who introduced me to political theory during my undergraduate days at Wellesley College—the late Ed Stettner and Roxanne Euben. Through their work and pedagogy, they taught me to think about politics in a different way. Anna Abulafia and John Marenbon, of Cambridge, deepened my love of premodern political thought and helped me venture into the world of epistemology and theories of knowledge.

This book began as a dissertation at the University of Chicago. Danielle Allen, Jacob Levy, and Patchen Markell helped me find and nurture this project and build a new intellectual life for myself. Through Danielle's own work and her engagement with my writing, she has shown me that the gulf between normative and historical approaches to political theory is not so wide after all. Since the beginning of this project, Patchen has asked me incisive questions about politics that have guided my thinking, questions that I am still struggling to answer for myself. Jacob encouraged me to explore the world of political economy in the long eighteenth century, a suggestion that set me on a path of inquiry I never could have imagined for myself. He's always a few steps ahead of me! That these three people remain committed to my scholarly development, as their lives grow even busier, is a testament to their good faith and good will as mentors. Every time I sit to write something, I imagine they are my readers. The intellectual community for political theorists at the University of Chicago is singular, and I would like to thank faculty and peers there who improved this project with their constructive suggestions: Andrew Dilts, Leigh Jenco, Jennifer London, Benjamin Lynerd, Mara Marin, Victor Muniz-Fraticelli, Michelle Murray, Patricia Nordeen, Neil Roberts, Nathan Tarcov, Deva Woodly, and the lively Chicago political theory workshop participants. I owe particular gratitude to Michelle Murray, who talked with me through many different versions of this project, and Neil Roberts, who read many different drafts of its chapters. Both of them have improved every aspect of my work with their characteristic intelligence, respect, and enthusiasm.

At Brown University's Political Theory Project, I found a new community of political theorists and philosophers who read my work and encouraged me to expand both my scholarly range and the depth of my inquiry. John Tomasi, Corey Brettschneider, David Estlund, Sharon Krause, and Charles Larmore were wonderful faculty mentors for a lucky group of postdoctoral fellows. Sharon has read and commented on different aspects of this project and has been a steadfast mentor and scholarly exemplar. I am grateful to my friends and peers at Brown who read and engaged parts of this book: Sahar Akhtar, Libby Anker, Jason Brennan, Barbara Buckinx, Yvonne Chiu, Leigh Jenco, Helene Landemore, Dennis Rasmussen, and Drew Volmert. Libby and Leigh helped me distill this project to its most important contributions, and Dennis has patiently read and commented on more versions of this book, and my other projects, than anyone other than their author. I'm extremely grateful for our intellectual camaraderie and exchange.

At Vanderbilt, I have found a diverse and erudite group of scholars immersed in social and political thought. I would especially like to thank my senior political theory colleagues Brooke Ackerly and W. James Booth for their encouragement as I finished this book, and for helping me think about how to make it as good as I possibly could. They have carefully read and commented on my work and pushed me to be as precise and bold as I could be in my scholarship. Additionally, they kindly organized a book manuscript workshop for me during a critical stage of revisions, and invited four scholars whose work has influenced mine: Deborah Baumgold, Jennifer Pitts, Dennis Rasmussen, and Andrew Sabl. The time we spent talking about this project were some of the best hours I have spent on it, and I thank all six of them for their suggestions, comments, and questions.

I spent 2012–2013 at Cornell University's Society for the Humanities, where I worked on this book and began a new project. I would like to thank Tim Murray for giving me this opportunity and creating an intellectual home for humanists who study risk. Tim, the other fellows, and the members of Cornell's political theory community made this one of the richest and most interesting academic years of my life. In the spring of 2015, when this book was nearly done, I had the pleasure of participating in a Folger seminar directed by Carl Wennerlind and Julia Rudolph, on the problem of capitalism in early modernity. The conversations among our seminar participants shaped my very last revisions of this manuscript and have given me a seemingly endless supply of questions and problems to occupy me going forward.

I am extremely grateful to the friends, colleagues, and teachers who have commented on parts of this manuscript and have had conversations with me about its questions and themes. I would like to thank (again, in some cases) Brooke Ackerly, Danielle Allen, Libby Anker, Barbara Arneil, Winifred Amaturo, Deborah Baumgold, James Booth, Ross Carroll, Doug Casson, Jonathan Caverley, William Deringer, Marc Hetherington, Jennie Ikuta, Kristy King, Dan Kapust, Sharon Krause, Jacob Levy, Paul Lim, Alex Livingston, Jennifer London, Ben Lynerd, Mara Marin, Patchen Markell, Michaela Mattes, Catherine Molineux, Michelle Murray, Christopher McIntosh, Victor Muniz-Fraticelli, Eric Nelson, Patricia Nordeen, John Parrish, Jennifer Pitts, Dennis Rasmussen, Neil Roberts, Jen Rubenstein, Andy Sabl, Stacy Clifford Simplican, Anna Marie Smith, Shannon Stimson, Megan Thomas, Jeffrey Tlumak, Michelle Tolman-Clarke, Brandon Turner, and Deva Woodly. Audiences at conferences and colloquia have also provided good feedback on several of this book's chapters, and have generated inspiring new avenues of research and writing: American Political Science Association, Association for Political Theory, Columbia University Political Theory Workshop, Cornell University Society for the Humanities Risk @Humanities Conference, Cornell Political Theory Workshop, George Washington University Political Science Department, Midwest Political Science Association, New England Political Science Association, University of Chicago Political Theory Workshop, University of Wisconsin–Madison Political Theory Workshop, Vanderbilt Social and Political Thought Workshop, and Western Political Science Association. Support from Brown's Political Theory Project, Cornell's Society for the Humanities, and Vanderbilt's Research Scholar Grant Program gave me the resources, time, and space I needed to complete this project. Beth Estes provided invaluable research assistance, and I thank her, too.

At Princeton University Press, I am indebted to Rob Tempio, who was the perfect editor for this book. He gave me essential critical feedback and insightful advice as I worked to complete it, and he also calmed my nerves at a critical stage of the process. I feel incredibly fortunate, especially as a first-time author, to have his guidance and help. I am also grateful to Melanie Mallon for her expert copyediting, and to Ryan Mulligan and Brigitte Pelner for their help with production. I would also like to thank the two anonymous reviewers who offered me incisive criticism and apt advice, as well as ideas for future projects, in their detailed engagement with my manuscript. Any errors or faults that remain are mine.

Friendship is one of the great gifts of my life, and I am so grateful to the people who have given me theirs: Karen and Greg Frost-Arnold; Michelle Murray and Chris McIntosh; Neil Roberts, Karima Barrow, and Kofi and Santiago; Bethany Albertson, Josh Busby, and Will; Michaela Mattes, Seiji Yamamoto, and Pax; Marc Hetherington, Suzanne Globetti, and Ben and Sammy; Liz Zechmeister, Andy Apodaca, and Natalie; Zeynep Somer-Topcu, Ufuk Topcu, and Atlas; Cecilia Mo and Yiaway Yeh; Brenton Kenkel, Brooke Hamilton, and Fiona; Catherine Molineux, landlady and friend, and Gromit; Marissa Guerrero; Jon Caverley; Monique Lyle; Jason Grissom, Dana Hughes, and Silas and Joy; the indomitable Ng sisters, Diana and Nora, and their lovely partners, Rob and John; Jennie Ikuta; Patricia Nordeen; Leigh Jenco, Perry Caldwell, and Casimir; Libby Anker, Matt Scherer, and Daniel and Lila; Bonnie Lipton and Paul Edelstein; Kim Priore; Michèle Mendelssohn; Mara Marin; Joanna Wulfsberg, Yucel Kuraoglu, and Kuzey; Victor Muñiz-Fraticelli, Michelle Cubano-Guzman, and Ignacio and Maria Cecilia; James Booth; Dana Nelson; Dennis Rasmussen; Chip Turner; and Jacob Levy and Shelley Clark. Frances and Sam Bethea gave me the greatest gift of my life when they conspired with my parents to rehome a dachshund/shih tzu rescue dog with me, right as I began revising my dissertation into this book.

I hope that my boisterous extended family know how much I cherish them and appreciate their support and enthusiasm for my projects. My brother, David, the best book reader I know, has rooted for me since we were little, and I depend on his steady influence. My sister-in-law, Katie, has become my dear friend and sister. And, my nephew, Isaac, is, in my unbiased opinion, the most wonderful child to walk this earth, and my favorite person.

My greatest debt is to my beloved parents, Habeeb and Cathy Nacol. They support me every day with their love and commitment, in both word and deed. This book, which is in some ways a study of how human beings struggle to learn about the world, is dedicated to them. All the really important things I know, they taught me.

AN AGE OF RISK

— CHAPTER ONE —

INTRODUCTION

How should we cope with risk? How do we confront a future that is, by definition, uncertain but still likely to contain *some* kind of peril or promise? Risk is an integral—and frequently uncomfortable—part of our daily experiences, an inevitable consequence of living in the world. As French philosopher and historian François Ewald explains, contemporary life is defined by risk; it is "in human beings, in their conduct, in their liberty, in the relations between them, in the fact of their association, in society."[1] The ubiquity and permanence of risk in our contemporary relations with each other and with nature make it hard to imagine that anyone has ever lived without it. But human beings once did, and thus the idea of risk has an origin and a history.[2]

Risk emerged in specific times and places as a new way of understanding the future and what harms or possibilities it might hold. In this book, I explore one site of emergence, to establish that risk developed as a new idea in seventeenth- and eighteenth-century British political and economic discourse. I interpret political theory and political economy from this period and place to show that risk became a meaningful concept for people trying to cope with the unknown, particularly in their political and commercial endeavors.[3] Accordingly, early modern British political thinkers developed critical accounts of the struggle to think about risk and to act on it, and they started to evaluate how its appearance transformed the forms and meanings of thought and action in politics and commerce. By the end of the eighteenth century, I argue, Ewald's diagnosis of the contemporary condition already held in Britain: political and commercial actors understood their conduct, relations, and associations in terms of risk. By then, risk was, to use his language, "in human beings," and thus a new age of risk had begun.

1

"Risk" and Risk in Early Modern Britain

"Risk" entered the English lexicon much as it did that of other European languages—as part of a technical, professional vocabulary belonging to traders and other commercial actors.[4] In the English language, the first known appearance of the word "risk" was in 1661, when it was defined, according to the *Oxford English Dictionary,* as a noun meaning "peril, jeopardy, danger, hazard, chance," reflecting an early and persistent association between risk and harm or loss. But it is worth noting that this early definition also included "chance," establishing an important link between risk and probability.[5]

As risk became a way for people in early modern Britain to describe what could lie ahead, a corresponding development in epistemology started to take hold. No longer a realm of fate, fortune, or providence, the future was conceived as a terrain of calculable risk.[6] In particular, probabilistic calculation—the basis of risk—began to gain traction in contentious epistemological debates about how human beings could best determine what an unknowable future might bring and how to respond.[7] The seventeenth century saw the production of the earliest probability theory texts, and philosophers and political thinkers also started to focus on probabilistic reasoning and the possibility (or impossibility) of acquiring certain knowledge that could guide decision making and action.[8] During this period, new forms of political and economic organization—centralized trading states, central banks, and insurance markets—also developed and consolidated. These institutions were designed expressly for coping with the uncertainties of politics and commerce as well as for managing a contingent future by conceptualizing it in terms of probability, prediction, and shared risk.

One of my major contentions in this book is that seventeenth- and eighteenth-century British political thought reflected these transformations and contended openly with the problem of risk.[9] In the following chapters, I concentrate on the contributions of four thinkers who offered particularly robust considerations of what risk means for political communities being transformed by new modes of knowledge production and by new institutions meant to cope with risk: Thomas Hobbes, John Locke, David Hume, and Adam Smith. I concentrate on Hobbes, Locke, Hume, and Smith because each of them produced a body of work that engaged deeply with different components essential to a rich account of risk. Although they were certainly not the first writers or thinkers to understand that the future was unknown and full of contingency, the aim of my study is to establish them as distinctive voices in advancing an idea of the future as a realm of risk. To do this, I take advantage of their polymathic proclivities and bring together their writings on epistemology, politics, sociability, and political economy to identify three important insights on risk and politics that should resonate with contemporary readers as well.

Scope and Summary

In chapter 2, I begin with Hobbes's intertwined theories of knowledge and politics, as they emerged from his experience of a violent civil war and fierce struggles over epistemological and political authority. As I argue, he provokes an early modern engagement with the concept of risk in politics by positing uncertainty as the main problem that political theory and political order are meant to solve. In *Leviathan*, Hobbes's construction of a unified sovereign power that quashes conflict is motivated by an epistemological obsession with the problem of uncertainty, and the primary aim of his civil science is to displace the conflicts created by limited knowledge of an unknown political future. For Hobbes, uncertainty is the root cause of violence and insecurity, and thus it becomes a target for elimination when he begins to think about how to construct a safe political community. In this chapter, I reconstruct Hobbes's commitment to a science of politics modeled on geometry, emphasizing its certain character by contrasting it with other ways of knowing about politics that are more experiential, such as prudence.

As I argue, despite his best efforts to construct a unified regime of certain knowledge production and absolutist political power, Hobbes's civil science is not capacious enough to cope with everything the future might bring. His heroic attempt to displace uncertainty from political life is especially important because of this failure, however. His thwarted efforts raise a valuable question, which sets an agenda for the thinkers who follow him: Can risk, suffering, and fear ever be truly overcome by political planning and more certain forms of scientific knowledge about collective life? Although Hobbes identifies epistemological and political uncertainty as a major source of political insecurity and suffering, his work leaves readers with the conclusion that uncertainty can never be displaced altogether. The thinkers after him turn to probability and judgment rather than certain knowledge as a resource for securing the future. This shift prepares them to think about the future in terms of calculable risk.

In chapter 3, I explain how Locke's work on epistemology, politics, and economy can be read as a sustained meditation on the relationship of risk and trust. The extensive literature on trust and authority in Locke's work establishes that he thinks citizens' trust in the state helps them organize and survive in the face of uncertainty, as well as manage the risks they might find in the future. In this chapter, I argue that Lockean political trust is actually more closely related to risk than it appears at first glance. Political trust, Locke theorizes, is actually underwritten by the perpetual work of risk calculation and probabilistic reasoning by citizens. His work shows that if a strong central state is the institution that manages political and economic risk for subjects, then those subjects still must scrutinize the state as a new risk, using whatever cognitive tools they have at their disposal. Locke's relative comfort with the permanence of uncertainty and his acceptance of risk as a part of common life lead him to theorize very powerful political authority and institutions as well as equally robust forms of citizen power, coupled in relations of trust.

To advance this interpretation, I analyze three particular episodes in Locke's corpus—two from his political theory and one from his economic writings: his concession to prerogative power as a necessary tool for the state; his reservation of the powers of political judgment and revolution for citizens; and finally, his engagement with the coinage controversies of the late 1690s. The first two cases in particular emphasize Locke's insight that profound uncertainty is the background condition of politics and commerce, as well as his insistence that probability and judgment are the best cognitive tools people have for cutting through radical uncertainty to perceive a more manageable set of risks. Locke's work also offers trust as a mode of confronting risks in politics and commerce, while remaining attentive to how risk underwrites trusting relationships, a point that the coinage controversy particularly highlights.

Chapter 4 offers an interpretation of David Hume's body of work as simultaneously sensitive to how uncertainty and risk can enervate commercial actors and committed to emboldening these actors to take *more* risks. I find in Hume's writings on passion, cognition, politics, and commerce an apt representation of how risk and uncertainty are entangled in the minds of subjects, as well as a robust explanation for why so many people are made anxious by risks, even ones that promise a good outcome. Hume's expressions of philosophical skepticism and his treatment of probability establish his view that deep uncertainty is the background condition for commerce and for the politics of commercial societies, and show that he is unusually mindful of the disconcerting experience of living with uncertainty. Although individuals can use probabilistic reasoning to formulate better understandings of the risks of an unknown future, Hume thinks this taxes them psychologically. Whereas thinking about the future can trigger hope *and* fear in individuals, he argues that in practice, it seems to generate *mostly* fear, even when people have stable probable beliefs about the future and well-founded expectations that joy rather than grief awaits them there.

After explaining how Hume reaches this conclusion, I explore the idea that his popular writings for a general reading public were meant as a resource for those who might wish to shake off the paralysis of uncertainty and the anxieties provoked by probabilistic thinking, at least to a degree sufficient to confront risk in commerce. Hume anticipates that members of a commercial public will fixate on both the probable and the improbable misfortunes introduced by complex and increasingly international economic exchanges. In his moral, political, and economic essays, Hume draws on his notions of philosophical proof as well as on familiar metaphors of stable natural phenomena to introduce the idea of a balanced system, in which risk taking in overseas commercial ventures produces profits in the long term and for the whole nation-state, while it sometimes hurts primary actors in the immediate term. Hume uses the conversational essay form to coax his readers into an attitudinal shift regarding risk taking, by reorienting them toward a measure of hope and optimism.

Finally, in chapter 5, I argue that Smith's moral theory and political economy confront human ambivalence about risk, by now a permanent feature of the human condition. Smith's analysis of individuals, groups, institutions, and policies leads him to find that human beings have a risk-loving side, which drives them to take chances to pursue gain, but that they also clamor to secure themselves against possible loss. How well they balance these two impulses can, Smith argues, issue in productive or dangerous approaches to risk taking. *The Wealth of Nations* records instances of a more pathological approach to risk, as Smith describes traders' corrupt manipulation of institutions, political networks, and policy to displace the responsibilities and losses that risk taking may incur. Smith's critique of monopolies and mercantile policies depends very much, I argue, on his view that traders exploit risk badly, by redistributing or jettisoning loss. Smith argues that those who pursue highly uncertain profits by taking risks in the political economy must also be willing to brook loss.

In his 1790 revisions to *The Theory of Moral Sentiments*, Smith draws a portrait of the prudent and trustworthy merchant, whose observable practices and character cultivate a climate of trust and predictability, which offsets the risks of trade without eschewing responsibility for losses. The prudent merchant's ambivalence toward risk tips him toward caution, and he supports his security-seeking endeavors with practical knowledge, reliable partners, and networks of trust and credit. Smith's call here for prudential approaches to risk taking at the level of individual actors may have been in response to an intervention from Jeremy Bentham, who counters Smith's pessimism about risk taking in *The Wealth of Nations* with the suggestion that progress is inextricably linked to risky endeavors pursued by bold individuals. Bentham's more sanguine views on risk may have invited further reflection by Smith on how commercial actors should approach risk, resulting in Smith's own modest but quite powerful intervention—a defense of the prudent man as the right kind of risk taker.

In each of these chapters, I reinterpret texts that are familiar to political theorists by arguing that we should look at them anew as significant contributions to emerging discourses of risk. At the same time, the thinkers I engage are distinctive, and their arguments are impossible to weave into a coherent whole or a progressive narrative about how human beings come to know more about risk and to improve their efforts at managing it. If anything, reading these texts together underscores how fraught and multifaceted early modern efforts to calculate and confront risk were. Yet, I argue, it is possible to identify continuities alongside important innovations in early modern British political thought on risk.

Dimensions of Risk in Early Modern British Thought

My interpretation of seventeenth- and eighteenth-century epistemological, political, and economic texts generates three insights into early modern British engagement with risk. First, we can spot a distinct conceptual refinement in late seventeenth-century sources, a development that carried over into the next century. Seventeenth-century epistemology and political thought was animated by the problem of uncertainty about the future, but by the eighteenth century, attention was more clearly focused on the problem of *risk*, as a matter of knowledge about the future that is rooted in conceptions of time, probability, and action. Curiously, however, even as we can identify this change, uncertainty and risk remained in something of a conceptual muddle throughout the eighteenth century—a confusion that we have inherited and that shapes our own efforts to confront an unknown future. While risk is conceptually distinct from blind uncertainty about the world and the future, it remains an uncertain form of knowledge.[10] Even though we can often be quite precise in our risk calculations, just the act of making these calculations may heighten the realization that we have to live with uncertainty. As such, we struggle to parse uncertainty and risk, and we even use the terms interchangeably at times, which strains our ability to make decisions for the future and to evaluate critically the efforts of authorities and experts to manage risk.[11]

The second insight this book draws out is the tight relationship between risk and trust in seventeenth- and eighteenth-century political thought and political economy. As risk is foregrounded as a problem for politics and commerce, the meaning and limits of trust in political authority and creditworthiness in political economy are thrown into sharp relief. Because the probable judgments of political and commercial actors are necessarily partial, and the future does not yet exist, these actors frequently need support in their endeavors. Networks and relationships of trust and credit frequently ease the way, emboldening actors to take more risks and perhaps even cushioning their fall if they choose badly. Conversely, trust and credit acquire meaning and value from the risks that underpin them.

Third and finally, the character of the political subject is worked out in the early modern engagement with risk, and the fearful subject emerges from this fraught process. At the beginning of the eighteenth century, the question of whether risk taking is exhilarating or threatening was still open. By the end, it had been established that even risks promising profit and benefit are painful to think about and to take, probably because the struggle to parse risk and uncertainty is such a persistent problem for individuals. This affective response to risk again underscores why trust and credit are so important for risk takers, as two of the few resources that help steel humans against the downsides of risk.

Beyond these three observations, I also argue that early modern British engagement with risk offers two narratives, views of risk that persist in our own time and shape our orientation toward an unknown future. First, I focus on accounts of risk as a threat to security; indeed, this is probably the prominent narrative of this book and of the risk literature in general. Negative readings of risk assert that marshaling our partial knowledge of the future will enable us to hold back from taking unnecessary risks or to displace the risks of politics and commerce as much as we possibly can. Second, I explore depictions of risk as an opportunity to be exploited for profit or gain. In these accounts, risk taking is figured as exhilarating or pleasurable, a chance to exercise freedom and choice in the interest of some gain. Even a cursory glance at the political or financial pages of a newspaper reveals the persistence of these narratives in our own time, and I aim to demonstrate that they emerged as soon as people started framing the future in terms of risk. Hence, these narratives have always conditioned our responses to a future that is not merely uncertain, but also risky.

At first glance, these two orientations to risk seem opposed, but they are in fact coupled in most of the key texts I interpret in this book. In some ways, this coupling is unsurprising—risk is not neutral, but it *is* indeterminate. It is simultaneously a threat to security and an opportunity for gain or profit because it is unknowable, except in a contingent or provisional way. Across the texts that are central to this book's analysis of the emergence of risk and of subsequent efforts to govern it, I find different iterations of the two faces of risk, in which one narrative is emphasized more than the other. I also find them linked in curious ways, such as in reflections on insurance, in which capitalizing on the risk of loss is quite profitable, or at moments when states claim outsized power to guard against the potential losses that subjects might suffer at the hands of disaster or war. Our ambivalence about risk taking, and our frequent inability to determine whether risks pose golden opportunities or profound threats, can be found in the earliest accounts of risk.

This ambivalence has serious consequences, as it may shape our choices regarding how to govern risk. In our own time, we are also frequently of two minds about what risk offers and equally uncertain about how it should be governed. We have the option to take an authoritarian approach to the production of knowledge about the future, informed by an endless search for security in the face of risk. Or, we can endorse a system that harnesses experience, intuition, flexibility, and a wider distribution of risk management. Our choices regarding how to articulate and cope with risk matter, not only in assessing risk accurately and facing it effectively, but also in the kinds of choices we make about knowledge production and the distribution of epistemological, political, and economic authority. We have not yet determined which paths to take, and this is why a historical perspective is so important. If we can recognize that our deliberations about what constitutes a risk, how it should be approached, and how it should be governed or managed are not especially novel, but as old as risk itself, we can reflect more critically on our own decisions.

CHAPTER TWO

"EXPERIENCE CONCLUDETH NOTHING UNIVERSALLY"

Hobbes and the Groundwork for a Political Theory of Risk

O n the heels of Thomas Hobbes's famous depiction of the "natural condition of mankind" in *Leviathan*'s thirteenth chapter comes an everyday example meant to secure the assent of his less scientifically inclined readers. Even after that chapter's detailed scientific analysis of the causes and logics of conflict in the absence of strong authority, Hobbes concedes that it may not yet seem obvious that people are thrown into a condition of profound insecurity without an absolute sovereign to rule them by law and force. For readers, however, a brief pause to consider their own daily practices should reinforce the veracity of Hobbes's scientific proof. Should anyone resist the implications of *Leviathan*'s account of the causes of war and its accompanying description of life under these conditions, Hobbes issues the following challenge:

> Let him therefore consider with himself—when taking a journey, he arms himself, and seeks to go well accompanied; when going to sleep, he locks his doors; when even in his house, he locks his chests, and this when he knows there be laws, and public officers, armed, to revenge all injuries shall be done him—what opinion he has of his fellow subjects, his children and servants, when he locks his chests. Does he not there as much accuse mankind by his actions, as I do by my words? (*L*, 13.10)[1]

This representation of the daily, perhaps reflexive or unconscious, habits of a prudent citizen points to the central pairing that motivates Hobbes's political theory of the state—the relationship between uncertainty and political insecurity. For Hobbes, life in an improperly ruled commonwealth is profoundly uncertain and thus feels dangerous, and this passage suggests that he assumes his readers also know this in a commonsensical way. Chapter 13's prepared citizen is not experiencing a robbery in any of the given scenarios, nor is he at all sure he *will* meet with harm. Rather, he is facing uncertainty about what will happen to him at the hands of his fellows. To cope with the fear and anxiety his uncertainty generates, he deploys assorted strategies to prevent the host of dangers he anticipates, perhaps based on unfortunate past experiences or knowledge of harms done to others. In other words, he is relying on an individual makeshift account of a fundamentally unknowable future as a guide for anticipation, action, and control.

The anxieties that haunt this particular citizen, this ordinary reader of *Leviathan*, are really not so different from those Hobbes predicts will affect all members of a poorly governed polity, one that is not held secure by absolute rule. This citizen's prudential practices suggest that, from past experiences, he has cobbled together the same perspective on common life that Hobbes aims to present with scientific clarity and rigor—that humans fear each another and feel compelled to plan for the possibility of harm and violence in the future. Both their own inexact prudence and Hobbes's more precise account of vulnerability and conflict can lead readers to identify the same challenge in the future—self-preservation in the face of uncertainty and deep insecurity. Thus in chapter 13, Hobbes draws attention to the confluence of two forms of social and political knowledge—the experiential and the scientific.

Upon further reflection, though, we can see that the mutually supportive relationship between Hobbes's scientific rendering of the natural condition and his representation of the cautious citizen is only apparent. A more careful reading exposes a real difference in the types of evidence Hobbes uses to mount his case. If we take chapter 13's example a little further, the armed citizen does not know with any certainty what will happen to him in the next instant but instead acts on the *probability*, or likelihood, that he will meet with harm. Hobbes means for the preceding account of mankind's "natural condition" to offer something more—a demonstrable argument for the *certainty* of conflict in the future. In the space between Hobbes's logical rendering of the inevitability of war in the absence of settled authority and his supporting example of the prudent citizen making his way through a presumably dangerous world, one important dynamic of *Leviathan* unfolds, the dynamic between forms of knowledge that are more and less certain. Hobbes's purpose is first to remind readers of their experiential awareness of their precarious positions and then to prove to them beyond doubt that they are indeed very vulnerable. He tacks back and forth between these two approaches to win assent for his intellectual and political project, even from those readers who do not share his scientific proclivities. If uncertainty and vulnerability are the background conditions of political life, then *Leviathan*'s aim is to construct a fundamentally knowable political order that can purge uncertainty, a commonwealth in which political authority and epistemological authority are joined and enforced from the top.

Leviathan's prudential citizen's ruminations and preparation for another night in the commonwealth are interesting not simply for their depiction of the fears that characterize political life. Chapter 13's vignette is also valuable for its particularly vivid renderings of uncertainty, probabilistic thought, and subsequent action—hallmarks of the problem of living with risk. I accordingly claim in this chapter that Hobbes was a critical early figure in the emergence of risk as a significant concept in seventeenth- and eighteenth-century British political writing. Throughout his corpus, but in *Leviathan* especially, Hobbes sets the elements of a robust consideration of uncertainty, risk, and political security in motion.[2] His study of political life is animated by a preoccupation with the problem of uncertainty and the struggle to acquire secure political knowledge for the present and the future. His work weds his concerns about the stability of knowledge and the stability of the state to generate a novel methodology for a civil science that can design and then support a regime that in turn quashes all forms of epistemological and political conflict and the insecurities these generate. In all of Hobbes's political work, but in *Leviathan* in particular, his efforts to construct a unified sovereign power that eliminates both kinds of insecurity and their consequences rest on his sensitivity to the problem of deep uncertainty.

In this chapter, I map Hobbes's efforts to secure the political future by reconstructing his commitment to a science of politics modeled on the methods of geometry, which he argues for by contrasting it with other ways of knowing about politics that are more subjective (e.g., experience, prudence, and history). Hobbes adopts a geometric method for his science of politics because he believes it allows him to present a certain, incontrovertible proof for a particular kind of absolutist political system—one that will adopt and buttress his preferred approach to knowledge acquisition in return. The idea is that proper scientific methods and absolutist political sovereignty can reinforce each other's authority to create a system without conflict. Ultimately, however, Hobbes's system of authority turns out to be quite fragile, revealing the futility of his efforts—or any effort—to displace uncertainty from political life. At the conclusion of *Leviathan*'s proof for a particular kind of state, in which epistemological and political authority are bound together, the problem of judgment still remains, a remainder that Hobbes may even acknowledge himself. I do not wish to insist that this is a flaw in Hobbes's argumentation for an absolutist state, although it might be. Instead, I suggest that by noticing how prudence and judgment creep back into the system that Hobbes designs precisely to avoid their influence, we are importantly reminded that uncertainty is an intractable problem for politics. Less-than-certain knowledge claims are, often, the only resources we have for political decision making and action.

Leviathan, and Hobbes's entire corpus, are thus of critical value if we want to understand the emergence of risk as a significant problem for seventeenth- and eighteenth-century political thought. His work raises a vexing question that, I suggest, sets an agenda for those who come after him: Can uncertainty, fear, and suffering ever be wholly overcome by political planning and more rigorous approaches to the acquisition of scientific knowledge about collective life? Though Hobbes rightly, I think, identifies the relationship between epistemological and political uncertainty as *the* major sources of insecurity and suffering, his work leads readers to the conclusion that uncertainty can never be excised from political life— neither by absolutist politics, nor by airtight scientific models for politics. Thinkers after him—for the purposes of this study, Locke, Hume, and Smith—take a different path and accept what he cannot brook. In their embrace of uncertainty as an immutable human condition, they turn instead to probability and judgment rather than demonstrable knowledge as resources for securing both political stability and economic profit. Hence, they are prepared to live with a future characterized by risk, in which thinking probabilistically about an unknown future is the only tool ordinary citizens, leaders, commercial actors, and political thinkers alike have for avoiding losses, ensuring stability, and even pursuing gains.

To support my claim that we should interpret Hobbes's epistemological and political writings as critical antecedents to more developed early modern accounts of the relationship between risk and politics, I examine Hobbes's body of work to recover his own struggle with the problem of knowing the future. In the first part of this chapter, I reconstruct the discussion of prudence that recurs in Hobbes's oeuvre, with prudence always figured as something of a rival to the particular mode of scientific reasoning he espouses, albeit a worthy rival that at times affirms or informs that reasoning. In part two, I consider the scholarly discipline that grows out of prudence—history—as a potential resource for political actors who must choose wisely in the present for the future. As with prudence, Hobbes approaches history with some ambivalence. Even as he appreciates its uses and indeed writes and translates histories himself, historical knowledge cannot displace uncertainty in the way that Hobbes wants, leading him to try other methods.

In the rest of this chapter, I evaluate Hobbes's solution to the problem of uncertainty in politics, at the levels of knowledge and practice—a civil science modeled on geometry. I explore the basis of Hobbes's preference for geometric approaches to knowledge production more generally, while asking whether such approaches can be properly adapted to fit the raw materials of social and political life. Hobbes's writings suggest that this relationship will have to work the other way around. That is, the raw materials of political life—people themselves—may find cause to adapt to civil science's contours and claims when faced with an absolute sovereign who oversees the production of civic knowledge and the management of politics.

Yet the lingering question is, what does this show us about the centrality of risk to his thought? Although Hobbes purposefully marries science and politics to build a certain future for individuals presently mired in political uncertainty, I suggest that his work is more interesting for what it reveals about the impossibility of such an audacious project, and for the remainders it leaves for those who also wish to contend with uncertainty as a core problem for politics and political economy. The failure of Hobbes's efforts, I argue, creates space for a turn to risk as a way of living with and moderating uncertainty.

Ways of Knowing the Future? The Limits of Prudence

In *Behemoth,* Hobbes's imaginative history of the English Civil War, he settles on the insufficient political knowledge of subjects as a main cause of the conflict, noting that "the people in general were so ignorant of their duty, as that not one perhaps of ten thousand knew what right any man had to command him, or what necessity there was of King or Commonwealth" (*B*, 4). He suggests that had the people been educated properly about both the necessity of political order and their responsibilities as subjects of Charles I, they would have been able to navigate the competing claims to authority by Crown, Church, and Parliament, and order might have been preserved. The failure of political order was thus traceable to a fundamental failure of knowledge.

The question of what counts as proper knowledge is perhaps *the* question of Hobbes's corpus, and a comparative study of the resources available for acquiring this knowledge is a thread that runs through his analysis of the human condition. In particular, the availability of reliable knowledge seems an especially urgent concern for politics, as Hobbes reflects in *Behemoth*. Without it, people are doomed to suffer, psychologically and physically, at the hands of others who also rely on partial or incorrect understandings of the political world.

In keeping with a long tradition in political thought, Hobbes scrutinizes very carefully the most immediate and personal resource that individuals have for guiding choice and action—the capacity for prudence they possess at birth. Significantly, however, Hobbes's account of prudence is largely divorced from robust consideration of it as a kind of virtue people cultivate, such as we might find in ancient treatments of prudence or practical wisdom, or even in later sources like Smith's *The Theory of Moral Sentiments*. Instead, Hobbes is mostly interested in the temporal dimensions of prudential thinking.[3] He primarily conceives of prudence along these lines, as an effort to imagine the future in relation to a known past. For him, prudence is a matter of conjecture based on experience or, more precisely, on careful consideration of patterns and signs that remain in memory from past experience. As he concludes in *Leviathan*, "when the thoughts of a man that has a design in hand, running over a multitude of things, observes how they conduce unto that design, or what design they may conduce unto, if his observations be such as are not easy or usual, this wit of his is called PRUDENCE" (*L*, 8.11). Making suppositions about the future or reconstructing the past based on patterns is no easy task, but all people develop this ability over time, perhaps even without much attention or concentrated effort.

Beyond Hobbes's emphasis on the temporality of prudential reasoning, his account of prudence also focuses on the cognitive work that constitutes it as a "wit." His definition of prudence in *Leviathan* identifies a basic human curiosity regarding patterns or relationships that could be used to predict future outcomes. This characterization does not, however, give much weight to what we might call the moral facets of prudence—conducting affairs with caution, planning carefully for the future with preservation and security in mind, and behaving responsibly with goods.

These dimensions are arguably present in the examples of prudential thought and action Hobbes gives, but his definition is strictly cognitive and focuses on the link between past and future.

In many respects, Hobbes's views on prudence presaged later accounts of probability that shaped the theories of risk in politics and in political economy put forth by thinkers like Locke and Hume, theories in which people imagine a future based on identifiable patterns culled from experience and use the resulting calculus to inform choice and action. As such, Hobbesian prudence can only yield partial and predictive knowledge of a future that has not yet arrived, even if that knowledge has a very strong chance of being correct. Its resonance with later forms of probabilistic thinking becomes more clear in the illustrative examples of prudence that Hobbes offers in multiple texts, culminating in the thin but precise definition he offers at last in *Leviathan.*

In an early treatment of prudence in *Elements of Law,* Hobbes uses the example of weather to illustrate the character of prudential reasoning as he constructs it, a model that allows him to reflect on the inherent limitations of prudence. If people see clouds, for instance, they are likely to expect rain in the future; conversely, if they see that it is already raining, they may surmise that clouds preceded the storm. In either case, these prudent observers are likely to be correct, especially if they dwell in a rainy climate and have witnessed their fair share of heavy clouds followed by rainstorms. Furthermore, they have a better chance of guessing correctly than people who live in dry and arid climates. Despite the ability of many people to predict the weather with some confidence, Hobbes stresses, they cannot conclude with certainty that clouds *always* bring rain, for "experience concludeth nothing universally" (*EL,* 1.4.9). This is partly because human beings cannot experience all there is, so people necessarily make unfounded presumptions about the future based on the partial information they do have. For those who have lived longer and observed more, prudence can be somewhat more reliable. People with more experience can choose how to act in the present with *more* certainty about future outcomes than can humans with little experience, but the major point for Hobbes is that no one can conjecture with "certainty enough" (*EL,* 1.4.10). Moreover, when making prudential judgments, all people, regardless of the breadth and depth of experience, access the past with some difficulty. The past lives in fading memory, and people also interpret these "faded" sense perceptions in the context of present conditions. Thus, the lesson imparted by *Elements of Law* is that prudence, while undeniably useful, can never be wholly reliable.

Hobbes does not deny that prudential knowledge carries significant weight for people as they move through a changing world. Yet, he stresses above all the contingent and limited nature of knowledge derived from experience and, therefore, the inability of the outcomes of prudential thinking to stand as reliable and certain truth claims.[4] This limitation of prudence has much to do with the partial character of experience and memory and thus is traceable to the thinking subject and his or her position in time. But, much of the trouble with prudence also lies with its object of knowledge—the future. Though depending on prudence may help people plan more successfully for the future than they otherwise might, no one can know with certainty what will happen there. The future by definition does not yet exist, and any attempts to predict it are at best tentative and provisional.[5] As Hobbes explains in *Elements of Law,* "No man can have in his mind a conception of the future, for the future is not yet. But of our conceptions of the past, we *make* a future; or rather, call past, future relatively" (*EL,* 1.4.7). While people make plans for the future from knowledge of the past, the future itself is marked by an absence of knowledge. Hence, even when people act prudently in hopes of fashioning a desirable future, prudence cannot insulate them from finding the unexpected there.

In some cases, the stakes of relying on contingent knowledge claims to plan a safer future are not terribly high, but Hobbes wants his readers to think carefully about the consequences of making social or political choices for the future armed only with prudence and experience. To revisit the example that began this chapter, of the prudent citizen who fortifies himself in anticipation of danger, we could wager that a careful man's precautionary actions harm no one, and that it is better for him to try to secure a safe future now than to be sorry later. The critical Hobbesian lesson, however, is that the future, despite its nonexistence, also shapes the present. When the cautious citizen acts with the future in mind, he transforms his social world in the process, now and later.[6] If he passes through the streets armed to the teeth or bolts his door, others who see him are likely to conclude that he has learned to protect himself based on his past experiences as the victim of violence or crime. To prepare prudently for the possibility of a violent future, he may unwittingly create a fearful and perhaps even less safe present, by silently modeling for others a need to anticipate the worst and prepare accordingly. Prudential efforts to reduce uncertainty are not merely feeble consolations in the face of an unknown future, then. More to the point, they are sometimes a bit *too* effective in the present, as they can create new, and undesirable, social consequences.[7] Hobbes thus suggests that social and political knowledge needs to be certain knowledge, because the stakes of confronting the future with anything less are simply too high in the context of present common life.

Hobbes proposes, therefore, that individual personal experience and prudential reasoning ought not to be the basis of truly authoritative knowledge about either the natural or the civil world. Individual prudence is, of course, not the only available source of knowledge, and people can and do search elsewhere for answers about how best to conduct themselves in the present while bearing the future in mind. In fact, Hobbes perceives the abundance of authoritative but conflicting sources of knowledge to be a problem, and part of his project in *Leviathan* and elsewhere is to evaluate the foundations of multiple intellectual disciplines—history and theology, for instance—to determine whether they can help human beings cope with uncertain conditions. He finds all but science to be deficient in this enterprise, and hence he tries to give science the last word on how social and political relationships should be studied and managed. The veracity of science comes to light not only in Hobbes's straightforward defense of it, but also in his analysis of its competitors.

The Uses of History

History is the collective and disciplinary counterpart to Hobbes's treatment of individual experience and prudence. A translator of ancient histories in his early career and a writer of modern ones in his later years, Hobbes gives historical knowledge some weight but is unwilling to endorse it as a *certain* guide for political actors. While it may help those who study it hone their prudential abilities, history can do little more than add to its reader's existing store of human experience. Although this is no small contribution, what matters for Hobbes is that history can never yield propositions that are universal and that can be followed confidently. History, like firsthand experience, deals in particulars rather than universal propositions that will hold true in every case. Hobbes's ambivalence regarding history as an authority or resource for political actors shapes his advocacy for scientific approaches to the study of politics and theories of political order, as we can see from his writings about history scattered across his body of work.[8] The relationship between history and science is not exactly a clean opposition for Hobbes, but he certainly minimizes the former in favor of the latter.

Hobbes defines "history" as "the register of knowledge of fact" in chapter 9 of *Leviathan*. Not especially novel, his definition confines the historian to dealing in the absolute knowledge acquired by sense and memory. The knowledge conveyed by the historian is "the knowledge required in a witness," which Hobbes distinguishes from the knowledge of the philosopher-scientist, who produces conditional, universal knowledge.[9] A philosopher engages in causal reasoning about bodies and their properties, either by working from a cause to its effect or by working from an effect to its cause. The historian's work is thus outside the scope of philosophy, because his "knowledge is but experience . . . and not ratiocination." Although Hobbes repeatedly suggests that history is distinct from philosophy, he still thinks they have a relationship, even insisting that history is "useful (nay necessary) to philosophy" (*DCo*, 1.8). The clear implication here is that history is subordinate to philosophy, but the claim that history is still *necessary* to philosophy provokes questions about whether philosophy's causal approach to knowledge production requires the added weight of experiential knowledge, an issue of concern later in this chapter when considering the limits of Hobbes's civil science.

The question of the status and value of history for politics persists in Hobbes's thought, and from his earliest writings. The preface and concluding remarks of Hobbes's first work, the 1629 translation of Thucydides's *The History of the Peloponnesian War*, contain particular words of praise for Thucydides and more general reflections on the merits and utility of a well-crafted history. In the text's dedicatory letter to William Cavendish, Hobbes offers his translation as a gift that he hopes will be of some practical use. He recommends Thucydides to Cavendish for "his writings, as having in them profitable instruction for noblemen, and such as may come to have the managing of great and weighty actions" (*TPW*, v). Shortly thereafter in the volume's preface, Hobbes suggests that all readers ought to value histories as critical tools that can help them choose their actions wisely, especially with respect to the consequences these choices bear for the future. He notes that "the principle and proper work of history [is] to instruct and enable men, by the knowledge of actions past, to bear themselves prudently in the present and providently towards the future" (*TPW*, vii). Hobbes's words to the young nobleman Cavendish, and to his readers in general, suggest plainly that people can depend on history as a guide for proper action. The careful study of history gives readers knowledge akin to that granted by experience, albeit knowledge that is secondhand and perhaps more dramatic in scope. Histories thus also create opportunities to make conjectures about the future and to choose wisely in the present, by providing representations of the outcomes of past conditions and events. The lessons offered in Thucydides's history are of the greatest importance to Hobbes—those on the origins of conflict.[10]

Since the purpose of reading histories is apparently the cultivation of prudence and skillful decision making in readers, it is unsurprising that Hobbes expects historians themselves to be people of exceptional intellectual virtue. In particular, he finds the best histories to be those written by scholars of good judgment who let the facts speak for themselves—to a point. The clearest statement of what he expects comes in chapter 8 of *Leviathan*, in which he notes that "in good history the judgment must be eminent, because the goodness consisteth in the method, in the truth, and in the choice of the actions that are most profitable to be known" (*L*, 8.5). Hobbes thus seems to give historians a fairly wide berth with respect to how they represent the past. They can, he argues, survey historical events and choose which ones to feature and which to obscure, according to what they think will profit the reader. Historians' representations of the past, then, ought to be colored by how they perceive the needs and demands of the present and perhaps those of the future as well.

The historian must make narrative choices with care and present them subtly, however, so that the text itself appears to do the teaching. Hobbes argues that *The History of the Peloponnesian War*, not Thucydides, teaches the reader some sharp political lessons about war and peace, and that this is the real mark of Thucydides's talent. The narration itself ought to lay bare its own lessons to the reader, and Hobbes notes that Thucydides is "yet accounted the most politic historiographer that ever writ," even though he "never digress[es] to read a lecture, moral or political, upon his own text, nor enter into men's hearts further than the acts themselves evidently guide him" (*TPW*, viii). Writing history is thus an intellectually demanding enterprise even, or especially, for historians who avoid polemic. They must choose an argument that is both manageable and significant for posterity; then they have the difficult task of carefully selecting which events to recount and in what order before representing them in their best prose (*TPW*, xxiv). The absence of the historian's voice in the narrative arc, however, is what makes a history great. Finally, for Hobbes, the use of history as a source of knowledge requires that the reader's intellect and judgment carry a burden, too. Because many historians either overtly or subtly inject their work with morals, manners, and policy to benefit the reader, the judicious reader must learn to separate the "contexture of the narration" from these "discourses inserted" (*TPW*, viii). Both writing and reading history require cognitive effort, a laborious parsing of facts, the careful construction and interpretation of narrative, and the exercise of prudential reasoning to distill the right lessons from the materials.

Hobbes's brief preface to *The Peloponnesian War* suggests that history, if done well and read well, can enrich decision-making capacities. A skilled and truthful historian has much to offer readers in the way of informative facts about the past. Perhaps more important, reading history cultivates the kind of rigorous prudential thinking about the relationship between past and future that promotes the performance of deeds appropriate both for the situation at hand and for a desirable future. Hobbes's praise for *The Peloponnesian War* as a superlative history suggests, however, that recording history, more than a simple reporting of the known facts of the past, requires a sophisticated understanding of what reading about and interpreting the past can teach.

Beyond what Hobbes writes to complement his translation of Thucydides's work and the faint praise for history we find in his philosophical works, we might also look to his own retelling of the English Civil War—*Behemoth*—as some evidence for the significance of the historian's contribution.[11] After establishing the causes and logic of war in his philosophical writings, Hobbes selects from the morass of facts about the civil war those "actions most profitable to be known" for his reader. Unsurprisingly, given his own interests, he focuses his attention on the problem of uncertainty and political judgment, and on the conflicts stirred by competing claims to epistemological authority. He chooses to document the proliferation of imperfect knowledge about political rule and obligation, as well as the state of popular ignorance about how to order the commonwealth. By Hobbes's own arguments, experiencing the spectacle of mid-seventeenth-century English politics cannot help *Behemoth*'s reader draw universal and certain conclusions about the causes and consequences of war that will hold in every case. But these experiences should mark the beginning of the reader's search for answers regarding the relationship between knowledge and politics, by prompting questions about what people need to know to stabilize politics—questions that the civil scientist can answer definitively.

History done well is thus suggestive of, or serves to support, what philosopher-scientists can go on to pin down conclusively with their work. While history might very well spur its readers to pursue scientific explanations for what they have "witnessed" on the page, by itself it cannot provide certain knowledge. Just as the man who arms himself and locks his doors may understand why he takes such precautions, readers of history may intuitively grasp why the events they study occurred and keep an eye open for resonant patterns in the present. But, historians and their readers cannot present a firm causal explanation for events that applies in all cases, Hobbes thinks, nor can the study of history alone help people make any real, definitive progress toward a future without the perils of uncertainty. History thus bears a significant relationship to philosophy and science, yet Hobbes claims it is no substitute, particularly when it comes to the project of eliminating uncertainty and securing the future. For that, he argues that people need a sturdier model.

The Geometric Method: Fashioning a Safe Political Future

In spite of Hobbes's insistence that the future must by definition remain opaque, his political projects remain assertively future oriented. His work suggests plainly that while efforts to know the future based on the past are inevitably constrained, humans do, in ways both purposive and unintended, continue to *make* a future for themselves. This is, in fact, the crux of the problem. Hobbes's analysis of both prudence and history reflects this insight, as he shows that how people interpret the relationship between past and future conditions their choices, and these decisions go on to create a new and previously unimagined future. Hobbes is sensitive to the uncertainty that hounds these efforts, as he catalogs the difficulties of sifting through conflicting information about or competing accounts of the past and present. His work is driven, then, by an effort to find the best means by which people can know and make a secure political future, free from the dangers of uncertainty. Hobbes attempts to solve this problem definitively at the level of knowledge by devising an error-proof civil science. He argues that embracing a civil science modeled on the methods of geometry will produce political knowledge that is atemporal and certain, ensuring in the process a certain and safe political future.

Hobbes figures science as an improvement on existing, less stable forms of knowledge production. In contrast to prudence and history, which are supported by inductive modes of thinking, science is a matter of proceeding from established first principles to deduce their consequences. As such, the knowledge it produces is conditional but universal: as long as conclusions follow from the set premises, they should always be true. Hobbes divides science into consequential knowledge of natural bodies and consequential knowledge of bodies politic, yet he favors one particular form of natural philosophy above all others and uses it to develop accounts of how to do all varieties of philosophy, including political.

The model for a scientific mode of philosophical inquiry is, as examples in *Leviathan* make clear, geometry.[12] To illustrate how people arrive at conditional and universal knowledge, Hobbes cites the following example: "We know that if the figure shown be a circle, then any straight line through the center shall divide it into two equal parts" (*L*, 9.1). Of course, knowing that a straight line drawn through the center of a circle splits it in half requires prior agreement about what a circle *is*, but this is Hobbes's point as well—to write a valid proof, a scientist must begin by defining the relevant terms.

The first business of a proper political philosophy or civil science modeled on geometry ought then to be determining "first definitions" and "signification of names," from whence scientists can go on to reason their way to a logical conclusion regarding the relationship of the parts in question (*L*, 4.12). Hobbes distinguishes reason, in fact, from other intellectual abilities, like prudence, in terms of this specific connection to language. He defines reason as nothing more than the "*reckoning* (that is, adding and subtracting) of the consequences of general names agreed on for the *marking* and *signifying* of our thoughts" (*L*, 5.2).[13] Scientists can know with certainty that their conditional statements are true always and everywhere only if they are definitive about starting points and rigorous in their logic. So, to render certain knowledge of politics, a civil scientist must be clear about defining the terms that matter for politics, the intentions and elements of the people who make up a commonwealth—a task Hobbes meticulously and energetically executes in the opening chapters of *Leviathan* and elsewhere. Once this difficult groundwork is complete, presumably civil science should be a matter of logic and proper reckoning.

One appeal of a scientific, geometric method of fashioning political knowledge over and against provisional, prudential approaches is its stabilizing effect on language. Hobbes argues that language, with its fraught connections to sense perception and experience, generates new forms of uncertainty and aggravates existing ones, in part because human practices of naming and defining perceptions are not uniform. A person's first instinct, Hobbes thinks, is to ground these practices in experience. Unfortunately, memory and experience, which are as diverse as the members of any community, are unhelpful starting points if agreement about first terms (and the certainty such agreement affords) is required. Early in *Leviathan*, he explains:

> The names of such things as affect us, that is, which please and displease us, because all men be not alike affected with the same thing,

nor the same man at all times, are in the common discourses of men of *inconstant* signification. For seeing all names are imposed to signify our conceptions, and all our affections are but conceptions, when we conceive of the same things differently, we can hardly avoid different naming of them. For the nature of that we conceive be the same, yet the diversity of our reception of it, in respect of different constitutions of body and prejudices of opinion, gives everything a tincture of our passions. (*L*, 3.2)

Hobbes thus diagnoses one of the root causes of conflict: when people try to communicate about their varying perceptions using words, they often end up operating at cross-purposes and come to intractable disagreement rather than mutual understanding.

The destabilizing effects of language are especially acute and troubling in the relationship between words and those ideas or conceptions that matter most for ethics and politics. The use of moral language is least constant of all, perhaps because its subject matter is also closest to human passion. As Hobbes explains later, an event that one person may describe as "just," another might call "unjust," depending on perspective, passion, and experience. People cannot, he thinks, use the moral or political terms they choose as tools to communicate effectively with one another, much less as starting points for reasoning out demonstrable proofs about the consequences of these terms for social relationships.

Hobbes thus speculates that the uncertainty generated by language is partly to blame for the breakdown of human relations. A situation in which people follow the uncertain dictates of prudence, or worse still, passion, and then struggle to communicate and justify their moral, social, and political choices to others, is not a situation conducive to peace. Put another way, people fail to use reason to formulate conclusions about proper political ends, and they fail from the start because they do not rightly define the terms such a scientific approach to politics requires. Thus they are left in a morass of perpetual disagreement and likely mutual distrust, with unreliable tools to settle the problem.

A science of politics, Hobbes argues, is critical to the polity's survival, since it offers a way to manage conflict by settling debates about the proper understanding and naming of the key elements of the commonwealth. These include human motivations and characteristics, as well as the building blocks of political society, such as rights, duties, and laws. In *Leviathan*, Hobbes makes the case for a geometric civil science as particularly well suited to cut through the morass of uncertainty caused by language.

But while Hobbes is committed to following a geometric model, thinking about politics is admittedly a more tendentious enterprise. As he documents so carefully in his body of work, even the most purposive efforts to plan for the political present and future, armed with experience and the wisdom of history, must rely on imperfect comparisons, changing meanings, and a society perpetually in flux.[14]

Although mapping the contours of political life via geometric civil science is Hobbes's best hope for combating uncertainty and confusion, even beginning such an enterprise is no easy matter. Hobbes duly notes that formulating *any* science of politics is especially difficult precisely because its subject matter affects people more deeply than much else does. In a thinly veiled attack on common law—another authoritative body of knowledge for political life—in *Leviathan* 11, he acknowledges something of a disjuncture between the basic materials of civil science and those of geometry, admitting how easily any effort to render a proper science of politics might be thwarted. He argues that when it comes to politics and social life, men

> appeal from custom to reason and from reason to custom, as it serves their turn, receding from custom where their interest requires it and settling themselves against reason as oft as reason is against them; which is the cause that the doctrine of right and wrong is perpetually disputed, both by the pen and the sword; whereas the doctrine of lines and figures is not so, because men care not, in that subject, what be truth, as a thing that crosses no man's ambition, profit, or lust. (*L*, 11.21)

Already, we see a suggestion here that fashioning a civil science will be politically fraught and difficult to remove from the field of passions and interests, whereas the appeal of geometry is that it excites neither in anyone. While this passage defends the geometric approach against other methods, it also draws out a potentially poor fit between geometric methods and the raw material of political life.[15]

Two critical questions thus remain: Can a science of politics be like geometry? Moreover, should it be? Hobbes raises these questions himself, and he answers both of them affirmatively, as he must. Even as he suggests that controversies over lines and figures differ from those over sovereignty and right, he insists that the method for arriving at conclusions that are true always and everywhere can and must be the same, whether this is applied to lines and figures or to passions and persons. His anxieties about the problems posed by both prudence and language suggest that part of the appeal of conceiving civil science as a geometric one is that doing so eliminates the uncertainty humans generate for each other when left only with experiential knowledge and an ad hoc and highly individualized moral vocabulary for communication. At the very least, he recognizes that a proliferation of competing forms of knowledge and unstable language contribute to discordant politics, and he believes that a geometric science could establish universal and true propositions and stabilize language. So, he thinks that applying the method of geometry to a study of politics is worth attempting, and further, that doing so might even be morally and politically urgent.[16]

The strongest statement of this urgency comes before Hobbes actually attempts to work out the proof himself in *Leviathan*. In the dedicatory letter prefacing 1642's *De Cive*, in which he develops some of the insights of *Elements of Law*, Hobbes explains why geometry is so admirable and relevant to his political concerns:

> The Geometers have managed their province outstandingly. For whatever benefit comes to human life from observation of the stars, from mapping of lands, from reckoning of time and from long-distance navigation; whatever is beautiful in buildings, strong in defense-works and marvelous in machines, whatever in short distinguishes the modern world from the barbarity of the past, is almost wholly the gift of Geometry; for what we owe to Physics, Physics owes to Geometry. If the moral Philosophers had done their job with equal success, I do not know what greater contribution human industry could have made to human happiness. *For if the patterns of human action were known with the same certainty as the relations of magnitude in figures, ambition and greed, whose power rests on the false opinions of the common people about right and wrong, would be disarmed, and the human race would enjoy such secure peace that (apart from conflicts over space as the population grew) it seems unlikely that it would ever have to fight again.* But as things are, the war of the sword and the war of the pens is perpetual; there is no greater knowledge of natural right and natural laws today than in the past; both parties to a dispute defend their right with the opinions of Philosophers; one and the same action is praised by some and criticized by others; a man now approves what at another time he condemns, and gives a different

judgment of an action when he does it than when someone else does the very same thing; all these things are obvious signs that what moral Philosophers have written up to now has contributed nothing to the knowledge of truth; its appeal has not lain in enlightening the mind but in lending the influence of attractive and emotive language to hasty and superficial opinions. (*DC,* epistle dedicatory, 6–7; emphasis added)

It is clear from this passage that Hobbes—enamored of geometry for its many contributions to modern life—rates moral philosophy quite poorly against other modes of inquiry. Though he has not yet told us how moral philosophers might approach the success of geometers, or how geometry might be brought to bear on political concerns, he clearly articulates the stakes of the problem. Doing civil science well, he suggests, is the only hope for peace. And the peace he envisions is not a temporary one. As we can see, Hobbes thinks that a good theory of moral and political life might put a permanent end to fighting, except under conditions of extreme scarcity.

As for whether civil scientists *can* devise demonstrable and certain proofs about humans and politics in the same way mathematicians can about angles and triangles, Hobbes thinks they can, and he works out an explanation in the decade that follows the composition of *De Cive.* The commonwealth is, he tells readers in the introduction to *Leviathan,* not a natural association but a matter of artifice—human making. The commonwealth's artificial, manmade character thus renders it a legitimate object of demonstrable proof, a position Hobbes also defends later in his 1656 *Six Lessons to the Professors of the Mathematiques,* a politically inflected document expounding the virtues of the geometric method.[17] There we find Hobbes's clearest statement of why geometry can and ought to be the model for civil science:

Of arts some are demonstrable, others indemonstrable, and *demonstrable are those the construction of the subject whereof is in the power of the artist himself,* who, in his demonstration, does no more than deduce the consequences of his own operation. The reason whereof is this, that the science of every subject is derived from a precognition of the causes, generation, and construction of the same; and consequently, where the causes are known, there is place for demonstration, but not where the causes are to seek for. Geometry therefore is demonstrable, for the lines and figures from which we reason are drawn and described by ourselves: and *civil philosophy is demonstrable, because we make the commonwealth ourselves.*[18]

Because Hobbes asserts that human beings make the commonwealth ex nihilo, he thinks it is entirely possible to know about its foundational parts and to grasp with certitude the logical interaction of these parts, just as it is possible to know a geometric proof to be true. As long as there is agreement on how to name and define the foundations of politics (namely, human beings, their characteristics, and their rights and duties), it is possible to reason about political ends and outcomes with certainty.[19] As Hobbes explains in his defense of the accessibility and universality of geometric proofs:

> All Doctrine begins at the understanding of words, and proceeds by Reasoning till it conclude in Science. He that will learn Geometry must understand the Termes before he begin, which that he may do, the Master demonstrateth nothing, but useth his Naturall prudence onely, as all men do, when they endeavor to make their meaning clearly known. For words understood are but the feed, and no part of the harvest of Philosophy.[20]

A parallel axiomatic proof about politics is Hobbes's project in *Leviathan*, and to a lesser degree in *Elements of Law* and *De Cive*. In these texts he attempts to define and name those aspects of human beings that bear significance for social and political lives, to treat his political-philosophical "harvest" with proper "feed," on the assumption that his readers will recognize and appreciate the veracity of his effort. From there, logical reasoning from cause to effect can take up the mantle:

> For as in the adding together of many and great Numbers, he cannot fail, that knoweth the Rules of Addition, and is also all the way so carefull, as not to mistake one number, or one place for another; so in any other Science, he that is perfect in the Rules of Logick, and is so watchfull over his Pen, as not to put one word for another, can never fail of making a true, though not perhaps the shortest and easiest demonstration.[21]

Through logical reasoning from agreed-on first terms, Hobbes tries to demonstrate how a civil scientist might painstakingly craft a true proof for the well-ordered commonwealth and thus put an end to uncertainty and ensuing conflict. If the definitions are clear, and the method is sound, then the proof can be replicated by anyone, or at least be understood.

Hobbes's argument for a geometric science over prudence as the key to acquiring dependable knowledge about politics rests on his assertion that the commonwealth is a product of construction and artifice rather than of evolution and nature.[22] Offering a demonstrable proof in geometry is possible because mathematicians generate the proof based on a common understanding of lines and figures. If Hobbes is right about the artificial character of the commonwealth, civil scientists should be able to offer a political theory of the commonwealth because they design the state themselves based on common understandings of its constituent parts. To be clear, this is a strong argument that geometry and civil science are homologous, and this position holds real normative appeal for Hobbes. A scientific approach to politics gets him what prudential approaches alone cannot—an indisputable blueprint for a secure political future, and by extension an opportunity to ensure the safety of subjects.

But, even if readers accept Hobbes's radical claim that politics is a matter not of nature but of artifice, it remains unclear whether they can then agree with his related assertion that the study of politics and the projection of a political future *can* be executed in the geometric manner he proposes. Accepting that the three angles of a triangle must always add up to 180 degrees is not difficult. The constituent parts of the commonwealth, however, are more difficult to ascertain and know, and the relationships among them are moving targets. In naming and defining the qualities of human beings—creatures of both passion and reason—Hobbes urges readers to recognize in themselves the representation of man to be found in the pages of *Leviathan* and to profess its truth.[23] Winning this agreement is utterly critical, because for Hobbes's political proof to hold any weight for his readership, there must be initial consensus about its most basic premises. This assent may not be easily won, for his points about the basic nature of human beings may not be so obvious. There is, indeed, evidence in his own work that his rendering of the essential terms of the commonwealth is perhaps more constructive and normative than merely descriptive at many points. The readers' experience of political life, and what they have read in experiential accounts of politics, may creep back in here to disrupt or challenge what Hobbes sets down so clearly in his texts. Not only that, this tension is present in Hobbes's work as well. To illuminate the discrepancy between political subjects as Hobbes defines them and as they live in practice, we might look to the frequently mentioned "problem of Essex," named so for a passage of *Behemoth*.

In *Leviathan* 14, Hobbes famously follows his depiction of the conflict generated in the state of nature with the argument that fear of a violent death drives human beings to seek peace. Fear of death thus serves as both an initial motivation to form a social agreement to exit nature and a durable basis for enforcing the agreement's obligation. To be clear, however, Hobbes is asking readers to recognize that his solution to the problem of persistent political conflict is viable *only* if another, less formal agreement precedes it: they must assent to his starting premise that fear of death is strong enough to trump all the passions that may lead to political conflict or anarchy. Hence, Hobbes expects fear of death to do quite a bit of work, both for his civil science and for the political arrangements that can flow from it.[24] This is not so troubling, as all of Hobbes's premises are key to his proof. But, in this case, the premise itself is controversial, as Hobbes's own work reveals.

In *Behemoth*, Hobbes makes a very brief mention of the Earl of Essex, who served as a general of the parliamentary armies in the English Civil War. On its own, this example is merely descriptive, but read alongside Hobbes's theoretical claims in *Leviathan*, it points to the instability of the fear of death as a reliable primary passion, or an essential corrective passion, for humans. Essex was famously twice-a-cuckold; the dissolution of his two marriages made him a subject of scandalous gossip for much of the early seventeenth century and hence a rather unpopular member of the court. As Speaker A recounts in *Behemoth*, "I believe verily, that the unfortunateness of his marriages had so discountenanced his conversation with ladies, that the court could not be his proper element, unless he had had some extraordinary favour there, to balance that calamity. But for particular discontent from the King, or intention of revenge for any supposed disgrace, I think he had none" (*B*, 112). This suggests that Essex marched onto the battlefield not to right any political wrong or even to defend himself or his cause against a perceived enemy. Rather, his motive was a purely vainglorious attempt to be recognized for valor and thus to soothe his own wounded pride and to restore his social status. Fear of death is trumped, in the case of Essex, by fear of something else—slander and shame in the eyes of the court and the public.

I do not wish to argue here simply that the Essex example puts too much pressure on Hobbes's proof in *Leviathan*, with the implication that paying attention to the real events of politics devastates his theory. Instead, I want to stress that *Behemoth*'s stylized historical example teaches us something about the tenor of Hobbes's proof in *Leviathan* (with the implication that the proofs of civil science can be and are politically and morally inflected). Hobbes is not merely scientifically documenting the foundations of commonwealth when he argues that fear of death motivates individuals to save themselves by making covenants and keeping them. Rather, he offers fear of death as *potentially* the strongest motive for avoiding conflict and seeking political peace. Because other passions generate political conflicts and motivate or sanction violent actions, fear of death is the one that he tries to stabilize and persuasively endorse via scientific argument in *Leviathan*. If readers are reasonable, he thinks they will recognize that their lives are not worth risking for reputation or other motivations, and they will opt to secure their bodies for the future by a mutual agreement to exit nature. The implication here is that Hobbes's account of human nature is not only descriptive or explanatory, and therefore not a matter of simply pinning down and articulating what readers intuitively know about themselves, as they might know a circle or a line when they see one. Rather, Hobbes is arguing for a very particular account of human nature, and one that requires assent—as I argue in this chapter, hard-earned assent—from readers before he can proceed to construct a commonwealth around it. Readers must accept how Hobbes defines them before they can agree to both the full proof for a Hobbesian commonwealth and any political manifestations of its depiction of authority and obligation. And sometimes, as the example of Essex shows, this requires accepting innovations that he is making.

But why do readers need to side with Hobbes on the finer points of human nature? Might they just move forward with his plan for an orderly commonwealth rooted in covenant and authorization and the related rights and duties these forms of political order require? If we place Hobbes's definition of reason from the early chapters of *Leviathan* alongside his reflections on the process of constructing a geometric civil science, we can see that the assent to first premises is essential. Before anyone can demonstrate publicly the consequential relationship among thoughts and perceptions, there must first be some agreement among the public on how these thoughts and perceptions are clarified, defined, and named. Ultimately, the production of certain, scientific knowledge must be a social enterprise, which sets it apart from the highly particular and relative character of experiential knowledge.[25]

Acknowledging the social component of scientific knowledge, in this case the knowledge produced by a civil science, is not to claim that Hobbes thinks that the naming of social and political concepts ought to be determined by the multitude, or that civil science is a project best conducted collectively. In fact, he suggests that popular efforts to formulate the right plan for the commonwealth have routinely failed, and that a singular intervention of the sort he offers is required:

> Though nothing can be immortal which mortals make, yet if men had the use of reason they pretend to, their commonwealths might be secured at least from perishing by internal diseases. For by the nature of their institution they are designed to live as long as mankind, or as the laws of nature, or as justice itself, which gives them life. Therefore, when they come to be dissolved, not by external violence but by intestine disorder, the fault is not in men as they are the *matter*, but as they are the *makers* and orderers of them. For men, as they become at last weary of irregular jostling, and hewing one another, and desire with all their hearts, to conform themselves into one firm and lasting edifice: so for want, both of the art of making fit laws to square their actions by, and also of humility and patience to suffer the rude and cumbersome points of their present greatness to be taken off, they cannot without the help of a very able architect, be compiled into any other than a crazy building, such as, hardly lasting out their own time, must assuredly fall upon the heads of their posterity. (*L*, 29.1)

As Hobbes portrays men in this passage, their status as makers of the commonwealth also positions them to destroy it totally. Here again, the problem is partly a knowledge-based one. In this case, because humans do not use reason properly to delineate the laws of nature, they also fail to formulate proper civil laws for the ordering of the commonwealth. The implication is that, left to their own devices, men rely on prudence, which they acquire with time and without rigorous intellectual labor. Prudence may help men formulate laws based on experience, but none of these will be universal or sufficiently stable to be fit "to square their actions by." Moreover, men are creatures of passion, a quality that also orients them toward the crafting of laws for personal benefit, but perhaps not for the good of the commonwealth. As much as they want peace, they are unwilling to "suffer" the blow to their pride and vainglory that a commonwealth structured by scientific premises rather than personal experience would require.

Subsequently, Hobbes does not suggest that men will come to the kind of reason such a commonwealth demands from them on their own.

Instead they must rely on an "able architect," who will not only build a stable commonwealth by himself but will also discipline would-be makers of the commonwealth into overcoming their passions and accepting the tenets of reason, namely the laws of nature. Surely the architect in question is the author of *Leviathan*, and the hope is that the text itself will serve as an event to break the cycle of uncertainty and the discord and violence it yields. The social character of knowledge, in Hobbes's account, is thus less about collective production practices and more about widespread assent.

The language of *Leviathan* 29 also recalls *Leviathan*'s early reference to another famed "crazy building," the Tower of Babel. In his account of the origins of speech, Hobbes argues that God was the "first author of speech," who bestowed the practice of proper naming of the animals on Adam, but the language humans received via Adam was lost when they erected the Tower of Babel and incurred God's wrath. Since that moment, the development of language has been an ad hoc enterprise, as people invent new terms according to need and by experience (*L*, 4.2). Thus the "able architect" who guides the makers of the commonwealth has a critical task prior to naming and promulgating the laws. He must begin by tangling with the problem of language, by settling the definitions from which logical argument must proceed. The need for science as a practice of naming and reasoning toward universal rules seems clear here, and the reference to biblical history reminds readers why, by revivifying the moment in which they created this need for themselves through hubris and folly (*L*, 4.1–2).

As the aforementioned example of Essex makes clear, Hobbes does not necessarily define the critical human elements of a body politic in ways that are immediately recognizable to his readers. The fit between the axioms he offers and the raw material of politics—human beings and their behavior—may not be an easy one much of the time. Still, Hobbes determines that pursuing a geometric approach to civil science is a worthwhile enterprise, regardless of whether this method maps cleanly onto the existing contours of political life. It is, he thinks, the only means to overcome the epistemological and linguistic uncertainty that underpins political conflict, and thus the only way to construct a certain and safer political future. Although Hobbes wants to wed geometry to civil science for these reasons, the benefits of arguing convincingly for his approach may ultimately flow in more than one direction.

The form of rule Hobbes ultimately recommends in *Leviathan* is one of absolute sovereignty, with one power that is the sole bearer of the ability to decide doctrine and to ensure that it will be taught. While agreement about first terms is essential to the scientific argument he makes for this kind of sovereign power, Hobbes is not optimistic that all will read and agree with his formulation, nor is he certain that it will defeat other, more experiential accounts of politics on offer. His political commitment to absolutism as expressed in *Leviathan* may, however, win him the agreement of a sovereign who is positioned to disseminate Hobbes's doctrine, and by extension, to secure his method and approach to political inquiry. As it turns out, the polity made by Hobbes's science may also need to be a polity made *for* Hobbes's science.

A Polity Fashioned for Science

Hobbes's initial worry about politics rests with both the ignorance of the people and the uncertainty and faction generated for them by competing claims to authoritative knowledge. After taking pains to establish a geometric civil science as the *only* route to universal knowledge, and hence as the sole path to a secure political future, Hobbes must address one more problem. Because he has genuine doubts about the ability of members of a commonwealth to rely on their own reason successfully, and perhaps a few suspicions that it may be difficult for them to agree to what he offers, the future of his preferred method for the production of knowledge remains vulnerable and at risk. A carefully formulated scientific approach to politics may not recommend itself to many readers. As he notes in *Leviathan*'s chapter on power, "the sciences are small power, because not eminent, and therefore not acknowledged in any man; nor are in all but in a few, and in them, but of a few things. For science is of that nature, as none can understand it to be, but such as in a good measure have attained" (*L*, 10.14). A scientific approach to politics may thus be doomed to obscurity; while essential to the survival of the commonwealth, it seems relegated to its margins—a difficult task that a few learned and somewhat marginal individuals set for themselves.[26] Hobbes hopes this will not be the case forever, and he anticipates that an absolute sovereign supported by his scientific proof is the best means by which to ensure the survival of his method, perhaps through public dissemination.

Hobbes makes an appeal to political authority in the introduction to *Leviathan*, expressing hope that the sovereign will be the first to assent to his scientific account of human nature and to the causal account of conflict and secure politics that flows from his prior definitions. As he claims:

He that is to govern a whole nation must read in himself, not this or that particular man, but mankind, which though it be hard to do, harder than to learn any language or science, yet when I shall have set down my own reading orderly and perspicuously, the pains left another will be only to consider if he find not the same in himself. For this kind of doctrine admitteth no other demonstration. (*L,* introduction.4)

Hobbes thinks that the text demonstrates nothing that the sovereign cannot already "read in himself," but suggests that *Leviathan* should spare him such rigorous introspection. Hobbes's aim is to win the agreement of the sovereign—who is cast as the first teacher of doctrines for the multitude—for Hobbes's political theory and, by extension, for his geometric approach to theory building. The sovereign in Hobbes's commonwealth is not only the arbiter of intellectual controversies but also the propagator of doctrine, who may "by good laws . . . encourage men to the study of them." Hobbes believes that if his doctrines were taught in universities, they would have far-reaching educational effects and eventually make their way into the doctrines of obedience and sovereignty taught to political subjects. As such, they might ultimately replace the prudential conclusions about politics drawn by the many (*L,* 31.41). While skeptical about the possibility that all people will perceive the merits of science and pursue the cultivation of reason with no prodding, he remains confident that the polity can be constructed such that the sovereign can educate the people to profess the truth of *Leviathan*'s teachings and thereby can generate a safe space for those committed to the practice of a geometric civil science.

Civil science and absolutist government thus exist in a tight and significant relationship in Hobbes's work. Because Hobbes thinks that a civil science modeled on geometry is the only means by which to draw certain conclusions about the political consequences of human passions and behavior, he holds it aloft as the only reliable tool people have for overcoming pernicious uncertainty in political life. At the same time, Hobbes recognizes the persistent threats to science in his social world. These two modes of conflict and threat—to the political community and to the scientific one—are of a piece. Multiple claims to authoritative knowledge is, in his view, one of the roots of political conflict. The polity Hobbes constructs must also be conducive to the longevity of his chosen scientific practices, just as his geometric civil science lays out a path to a durable commonwealth. With an absolute sovereign in place, who selects and disseminates doctrine, science's rivals for the claim to authoritative knowledge can be rejected, as long as Hobbes makes his case for a geometric science as the means to political stability and support for absolute sovereignty. If he can persuade the sovereign that his geometric political proof displaces all uncertainty about political obligation and hence all chance of political resistance, he may be able to preserve simultaneously the method of procuring political knowledge that he is unwilling to leave to chance—a geometric civil science.

We must sit with the question of where this leaves Hobbesian subjects, however. In the process of undermining reliance on ordinary approaches to fashioning a more certain political future, Hobbes has required very little cognitive work from political subjects, to whom he assigns meager epistemological authority. He has, however, placed heavy political demands on them, suggesting that their primary role in politics is to assent to unified epistemological and political authority, located in the seat of the sovereign. The covenanting subject of *Leviathan* 14 seems less significant on this reading, which stresses the essential role of the authorizing, assenting subject of *Leviathan* 17.[27] While Hobbes has arguably worked to improve the political lot of all people in his efforts to reduce uncertainty and conflict in politics, his account also builds a powerful alliance between a very particular subset of the scientific community and an indivisible sovereign, a partnership against which the modes of resistance are few.

Traces of Prudence? The Limits of Civil Science

Hobbes's effort to fuse absolutist politics with a unified system of knowledge production modeled on geometry turns out to be quite fragile, in ways already suggested in this chapter. As the discussion of how Hobbes settles the principles of his civil science implies, it is not clear who has the final word on the definitions he offers as the foundation of the civil science that flows from them: The reading public, with its prudential intuitions about who the natural man is? Another expert civil scientist like Hobbes? A sovereign who holds both epistemological authority and a monopoly on legitimate force? While Hobbes postulates that the union of all these potential sources is the most secure route, perhaps beginning with an alliance between civil science and the state, it is just as likely that tension among them might fracture the unified edifice of Hobbes's political-epistemological order.

Hobbes's personal and political struggles to secure his method against scientific alternatives have been well documented, but ample evidence for the unsteadiness of his system appears within *Leviathan* as well.[28] Specifically, Hobbes's work raises and even repeats a question that his account of a geometric civil science can never quite settle. Is a science of politics enough, or must experience come back into political decision making at critical points?[29] Connected to this question is another of critical importance: If science requires the help of experience, how are these competing ways of knowing the future ordered or prioritized, such that political life does not spin back into disorder and uncertainty? In *Leviathan*'s chapter on counsel, we find one clue.

In chapter 25 of *Leviathan*, Hobbes notes that sovereigns will likely require some good counsel, and so he sets about distinguishing binding commands from counsel and advice and enumerating the qualities of good counselors. Though he has taken great pains to insulate his political system from the uncertain claims of prudential approaches to politics, prudence recovers some political ground in this chapter. The sovereign certainly has final say over political decision making, but the chapter on counsel suggests that he does not have a total monopoly on political knowledge. At the very least, advisers who draw on prudence and experience influence his decisions.

The primary role of the counselor is to make clear the consequences of any political decisions or actions the sovereign might take. The standards for counselors' presentation and argumentation before the sovereign are very high, and in some respects, they map onto Hobbes's account of what a geometric science of politics can do. Hobbes argues that the counselor must "propound his advice in such form of speech as may make the truth most evidently appear, that is to say, with as firm ratiocination, as significant and proper language, and as briefly as the evidence will permit" (*L*, 25.12). The counselor must take care to eliminate from his speech any "rash and unevident inferences" that draw on eyewitness accounts, opinion, or examples from books; likewise, he must purge his speech of any "obscure, confused, and ambiguous expressions, also all metaphorical speeches" that might stir the passions and interfere with the formation of reasonable arguments (*L*, 25.12). Thus far, the work of the counselor seems to be at one with the kind of argument a civil scientist such as Hobbes would make. Hobbes's account of counsel does not do much yet to disrupt the picture of a political world in which sovereign and civil science are unified and counselors follow suit.

Immediately thereafter, however, Hobbes suggests that true skill as a counselor comes from another source—experience and reflection, the hallmarks of prudential thought and the building blocks of history done well. He notes that the capacity for counsel is only developed by experience and careful study, and "no man is presumed to be a good counsellor, but in such business as he hath not only been much versed in, but hath also much meditated on, and considered." As the purpose of the commonwealth is to preserve peace domestically and defend against outside invasion, the sovereign requires counsel from those who have "great knowledge of the disposition of mankind, of the rights of government, and of the nature of equity, law, justice, and honour (not to be attained without study)." Presumably, much of this knowledge can be procured directly from engaging a rigorous civil science like Hobbes's. But counselors must also know "of the strength, commodities, places, both of their own country, and their neighbours, as also of the inclinations and designs of all nations that may any way annoy them." This kind of very particular, context-specific knowledge is "not attained to without much experience" in the field and the use of judgment to reflect on the meaning and significance of experience (L, 25.13).[30] Ideally, the sovereign will assemble a range of counselors who are experts in different areas of significance to a ruler and will gather and mull over their expert advice before choosing a course of action that will best secure the longevity of the commonwealth for the future.

Significantly, Hobbes suggests that the best counselors will draw on both science and experience for knowledge. In some cases, good advice will come from knowledge of universal, certain rules. As Hobbes writes, "When for the doing of anything there be infallible rules as in engines and edifices, the rules of geometry, all the experience of the world cannot equal his counsel that has learnt or found out the rule." In these cases, political expertise is a matter of knowing the rules developed by scientific investigation and reason. But this is not enough, it would seem. Hobbes concludes, "And *when there is no such rule*, he that hath most experience in that particular kind of business has therein the best judgment, and is the best counselor" (L, 25.13; emphasis added). In some cases, then, there is no rule for proceeding in politics, no certain guide for securing the future. Expertise, in this case, is a matter of judgment and experience, a manifestation of the prudence that Hobbes compares unfavorably with the certainty of science elsewhere. Moreover, this admission suggests that the question of expertise in politics is open—while the sovereign may have final say, it is not clear whether the civil scientist or an expert of some other kind will be the one to provide the necessary knowledge. Here we can see a slight opening in the tight regime of knowledge and political authority that Hobbes posits as the only way to a certain future for the commonwealth and its people. Though this is but a brief example from one text, it suggests strongly that politics requires, even for Hobbes, multiple ways of proceeding into an unknown future, and it raises the question of how different modes of knowledge production can be prioritized or ordered within the commonwealth.[31]

To be clear, I do not introduce Hobbes's views on counsel to suggest that his civil science and the state it supports are poorly constructed and thereby doomed to fail each other. Rather, my point is that the alliance between civil science and the state is not enough, and Hobbes seems to have known as much. A Hobbesian sovereign must still, it seems, face contingent or unexpected events, because these are simply persistent features of the political world, an insight Locke will formulate even more clearly a few decades later. In politics, there are events or circumstances for which there is no definition or rule of thumb, and here experience and prudential conjecture become important again. Put another way, uncertainty cannot be removed, and more tools are required than a geometric science of politics to confront it.

Conclusion

In this chapter, I argue that Hobbes's work, especially *Leviathan*, provides especially fruitful material for thinking about uncertainty as a persistent condition for human beings and as *the* problem to be solved by theorists of politics. Hobbes's engagement with and questioning of the limited benefits of prudence and experiential knowledge establish that the impossibility of conceptualizing the future is a source of anxiety, suffering, and—more significantly for politics—interpersonal and violent conflict. Hobbes locates the highest stakes of politics at the level of the procurement of knowledge. He suggests that political problems are often grounded in basic knowledge problems, an insight that figures importantly in the work of the other authors central to this book, as well as in scholarship on risk and politics. Politics is an uncertain, risky, and dangerous enterprise because human beings are not sufficiently equipped with what they need to know. In particular, Hobbes thinks that individuals have no understanding of what being a good subject entails—a problem that stems both from the inherent limitations of humans as thinking bodies and from a dearth of reliable sources from which to learn.

Hobbes aims to rescue political life from the inexact character of ordinary knowledge and from feuding communities of experts—theologians, experimental scientists, and politicians—by modeling an authoritative and decisive political theory on geometry, the most accessible and methodologically airtight of the sciences. While no admirer of popular wisdom or public reason, Hobbes expects that any person with reason should be able to grasp the validity of a political theory constructed as an axiomatic proof. The ability of subjects to consent is a key element of Hobbes's theory of politics, for indeed they must be able to consent to form a covenant in the first instance and to authorize a sovereign in the next. But the public of political subjects must be Hobbes's readers even before this, it seems, and must assent to his formulation of human beings and his method for determining how a polity ought to be constructed. A civil science, delivered in the form of *Leviathan*, teaches and disciplines by requiring such assent; the scientific text itself is the intervention necessary for creating a secure state that can in turn establish science and the knowledge it produces as authoritative.

Hobbes thus offers a geometric approach to thinking about politics as the best means of managing the dangers and harms of political life, nearly all of which are rooted in uncertainty. The shortcomings of experience and prudence are thrown into relief by his evaluation of science as a means of solving the knowledge problems that bring conflict to politics. He argues that science is the only means by which people can acquire certain and indisputable knowledge of who they are, why their politics are disorderly, and how they can maintain order for the future. By generating axioms and reasoning from these principles to certain conclusions, a geometric civil science is able, he thinks, to offer a secure political future in the form of absolutist order. Hobbes develops his cases for absolutism and a science of politics side by side, and he argues persistently for the unification of natural and civil science and the protection of both by a sovereign. In the process of establishing the primacy of science, he also reveals that knowledge ought not be left to chance in the political arena. As he writes at the conclusion of part 2 of *Leviathan*, "I recover some hope that, one time or other, this writing of mine may fall into the hands of a sovereign who will consider it himself . . . without the help of any interested or envious interpreter, and by the exercise of entire sovereignty in protecting the public teaching of it, convert this truth of speculation into the utility of practice" (*L*, 31.41). The polity Hobbes generates depends on geometric science for its design and justification. In turn he expects that polity to protect the primacy of geometry as the authoritative path to knowledge by holding up *Leviathan* as an exemplary civil science.

But, even Hobbes's own work implies the vulnerability and partiality of his system, as when he considers the ways prudence and counsel make their way back into the search for political knowledge. It would seem that the assumptions, theorems, and proofs about politics so carefully mapped in *Leviathan* are not enough; there will be, Hobbes admits, contingencies in political life that will reveal the fixed and subsequently brittle nature of his civil science. These events will demand confrontation, with only partial, uncertain experiential knowledge in hand. Hence, at points *Leviathan* suggests that uncertainty—and the suffering and vulnerability that Hobbes thinks come with uncertainty—can never be displaced from politics altogether.

While the insights of his work stand on their own, I argue that Hobbes also opened up other avenues for early modern thinkers who were starting to formulate questions about uncertainty and risk. His rich consideration of prudence, a way of knowing the future that he criticizes and subordinates in favor of the certainty of geometric science, becomes more critical and central for others who take up the project of knowing and coping with a future that does not yet exist. For Locke, uncertainty becomes the most permanent feature of politics and political economy, a condition that can only be managed by probabilistic reasoning and good judgment. Hume and Smith also take uncertainty as a given and caution seriously against the kind of totalizing system that Hobbes builds to displace it. Although Hobbes's approach to securing the future fell out of fashion almost immediately, he must still be read as an agenda-setting thinker for early modern British engagements with the problems of uncertainty and risk. In his struggle to find reliable knowledge for an unknown future, and to secure knowledge production politically, he places uncertainty in the foreground of political thought and raises the question of the relationship between certain knowledge and political security, a question that holds priority for theorists of risk.

CHAPTER THREE

THE RISKS OF
POLITICAL AUTHORITY

Trust, Knowledge, and Political Agency
in Locke's Politics and Economy

In this chapter, I focus on the interplay of trust and risk in John Locke's body of work, by beginning and ending with the question of how Locke thinks people can acquire reliable political and economic knowledge. We can read Locke's epistemological works, especially *An Essay Concerning Human Understanding*, as a serious warning to readers not to take too much knowledge on trust, but instead to scrutinize carefully what they think they know. Despite this cautionary stance, when he considers the question of how political subjects can cope with the persistently uncertain character of political life, Locke turns to trust as a productive resource. In particular, he deploys the legal metaphor of a fiduciary trust as a model for political authority and obligation. Locke's insistence that both subjects and rulers should embrace a fiduciary model for political relations does not mean that the quest for better and more precise knowledge ends with this choice, however. Locke's turn to trust instead emphasizes even more boldly the dangerous stakes of knowledge acquisition in matters of political and commercial life, particularly for political and economic subjects. It leads him to encourage vigilance, surveillance, and judgment in those who do the entrusting. As beneficiaries of political trust, Lockean subjects are charged with the thorny intellectual task of determining when their rulers have defrauded them or are no longer capable of protecting their interests and goods. Locke stresses that trustees must be perpetually scrutinized as objects of knowledge if subjects are to offset the risks of relying on a trust to make political relations productive and good.

By emphasizing that risk is "the very essence of trust," Locke's work does much more than offer an account of trust as a resource for politics and a depiction of a network of interpersonal relationships that characterize a flourishing society.[1] It also captures in a nuanced way the shifting power relations and asymmetries that characterize all trusting relationships, and it offers the insight that we often best understand what trust entails retroactively—that is, when it is already broken beyond repair or when it is so strained that it might snap.[2] To know what trust is and what it means for politics, we must acknowledge its tight relationship to risk, as well as to the myriad knowledge problems that shape political life. In this chapter I argue that this cluster of observations about risk and trust are the core contributions of Locke's political theory to seventeenth- and eighteenth-century discourses of uncertainty, probability, and risk, and that they bear implications for his views on political economy as well.

Locke's work presents a significant development in early modern British thinking about risk and how to govern it. In contrast to Hobbes's reluctance to accept uncertainty as an intractable feature of political life, Locke acknowledges uncertainty and deep vulnerability as permanent background conditions for political and economic endeavors. His question becomes not how to displace uncertainty but how to temper or manage it effectively through the use of well-honed judgment and properly constructed political arrangements.

Locke's work thus represents a significant reorientation to the problem of uncertainty, one that holds steady through eighteenth-century efforts to acquire knowledge of the risks of politics and of political economy. Locke's epistemology, political thought, and policy considerations on money and political economy offer something new. Specifically, I argue that Locke accepts uncertainty and uses the tools of probabilistic knowledge to start conceiving the future in terms of calculable risk. Paradoxically, Locke brings novelty to and advances knowledge about how to face the risks of the future by returning to resources from the past. He turns away from the innovative, radical forms of certain political knowledge that Hobbes had been developing and endorsing, and looks back to older, less certain forms of knowledge, rooted in experience, prudence, and probability. This intervention turns out to be quite powerful, and we will see its manifestations in eighteenth-century approaches to uncertainty and risk, too.

In the first section of this chapter, I elaborate the claim that Locke understands political life to be characterized by accidents, contingency, and uncertainty, all of which threaten the central political goal of protecting the common good. While he does not depict uncertainty as a good thing for politics, he accepts it as a background condition for common life, and one that will never be wholly displaced. Although, like Hobbes, Locke devises a compact among subjects as one significant means of regulating or diminishing the uncertainties of common life, his work (again, in keeping with Hobbes) offers a still more robust means of coping with flux—modeling relations of political authority and rule on the practice of fiduciary trust. The trust model Locke endorses is appropriately open and flexible, as perhaps any tool must be that copes with contingency, variability, and the uncertainty and risks they pose. The elasticity of the trust also contains, however, the potential for both profitable political relations and profound betrayal. A fiduciary trust can be either a means of security and benefit or a source of insecurity and loss; it holds the seeds of both, as all risks do. Thus when trust is used to govern the risks of common life, it becomes a risk itself. Locke's work therefore underscores the permanent character of risk as a phenomenon that, once introduced, can never be displaced. Even efforts to manage it can issue in new fields of risk to be scrutinized and treated as objects of probable knowledge.

In this chapter, I analyze a pair of countervailing episodes in Locke's political thought that illustrate the two-sided character of trust and risk, as well as the permanence of risk. First, I consider briefly Locke's account of prerogative power as an illustration of the useful flexibility of the trust model. The holder of prerogative, as a trustee of the people's good, has a special capacity to cope with political contingencies as they come, predominantly through the exercise of judgment. That is, Locke figures prerogative as a critical tool that helps the body politic confront both uncertainty and risk, and its status as a singular power makes it uniquely useful for coping with sudden or looming problems. Because of its exceptional character, however, prerogative is also particularly open to abuse, and it subjects citizens to a potentially overwhelming power that demands constant scrutiny for signs of broken or abused trust. Thus, even as Locke endorses prerogative as a necessary corrective to the vicissitudes of political life, he is well aware that it places a strain on trust and makes serious cognitive demands on trustees. As such, prerogative illuminates the dual character of Lockean trust as a risk, with emphasis on its darker register—it is a source of stability against the unexpected, but it generates insecurity and stands as a potential threat itself.

I then examine the conceptual counterweight Locke puts in place against prerogative—popular resistance. Locke's work on revolution raises a critical question of when and how subjects can know that the risks of political trust have become too much to bear. Locke offers two ways of knowing, beginning with the most certain: sensory and experiential knowledge. He suggests that people can see with their eyes and feel with their bodies that their once trustworthy rulers have become tyrants or abusers. So, it would seem that broken trust is obvious, and that trust itself requires little more than a passive orientation to political power and an acquisition of knowledge that comes almost involuntarily. But Locke, albeit briefly, also poses a challenge to his own point: he argues that subjects must be able to resist before they acquire *certain* knowledge of tyranny, which may come too late.[3] I suggest that probabilistic reasoning, which Locke theorizes in his epistemological writings, is another tool subjects have at their disposal to evaluate the effectiveness and aims of the powers to which they have entrusted their lives and goods. More strongly, I argue that it is the most politically critical resource subjects have. If we take Locke's argument for preemptive revolution seriously, then it turns out that a scrutiny akin to risk calculation is both a strong basis for the generation of popular power and a task to be performed continually in politics by the beneficiaries of a political trust.

This chapter demonstrates that Locke's theory of political authority, as a formal trust relationship that structures political life, depends on a prior view of citizens as embodied, thinking subjects who can reason probabilistically as much as it depends on his understanding of uncertainty as a persistent human condition. Locke also offers an account of political subjecthood and agency that emphasizes the role of cognition and thought as well as action, a perspective that is so important for the study of risk. Reading Locke's account of trust as a potential resource for understanding early modern views on risk thus draws out two significant developments. It endorses for politics the probabilistic reasoning that is crucial to conceptualizing the future in terms of risk rather than sheer uncertainty, and it suggests that uncertainty and risk are conditions to be lived with rather than displaced.

Locke himself knew this quite well from a practical political standpoint. Although I devote most of this chapter to investigating how Locke's epistemology figures into his rendering of political relationships and practices, he was also both a theorist and a practitioner of political economy, which posed a distinct but related set of risks for the state and the public. This chapter thus concludes with something of a dismal coda, one that prefigures the kinds of reflections Hume and Smith will offer on the pervasive risks of political economy. In the 1690s, several years after Locke's thoughts on probability and political trust went into print—some works attributed directly to him and some published anonymously—he became involved in efforts to manage an impending monetary crisis triggered by corrupt merchants who were clipping coins. Locke's reflections on the coinage crisis, taken from his pamphlets on money and interest, point to the fragility of trust and the ongoing problem of risk in a fledgling commercial state. In fact, Locke's economic writings contain the few instances in which he writes about risk directly, although my argument in this chapter is that his entire body of work theorizes the risks of trust.

The efforts of coin clippers to destabilize currency and defraud the public put a clear strain on the public trust and the public good. Currency fraud struck right at the heart of exchange between subjects; it thwarted efforts to get a reliable grip on exchange value and to plan commercial transactions, and it thus threatened commercial exchange, a practice that depends on trust. Locke's engagement with the coinage problem, and his effort to solve it as a participant in government, reflect the kinds of ongoing epistemological, political, and economic crises that challenge a state and its citizenry and thus give us another dimension of his thought on uncertainty, risk, and trust. Moreover, for the purposes of this book, Locke's work on the coinage crisis presaged the kinds of troubling orientations to risk that both Hume and Smith would find among the merchant classes, figures of political and commercial power and influence in the eighteenth century.

Flux, Unpredictability, and the Protection of a Common Good

Locke's attention to the complexity and contingency of social, political, and economic life draws out what he thinks is most at risk—the common good. Just before offering a defense of prerogative power in the *Second Treatise of Government*, he articulates what he takes to be the shared practical problem of peoples and their governments—how to keep political communities stable and even flourishing despite unpredictable and changing circumstances.[4] As he explains:

> Things of this World are in so constant a Flux, that nothing remains long in the same State. Thus People, Riches, Trade, Power, change their Stations; flourishing mighty cities come to ruine, and prove in time neglected desolate Corners, whilst other unfrequented places grow into populous Countries, fill'd with Wealth and Inhabitants. (*ST*, 157)[5]

Though this passage is a pointed reflection on the specific political problem of rotten boroughs, it gives us a window into Locke's broader views on the human condition. Locke is a thinker who acknowledges and even accepts both uncertainty and contingency as part of life and politics, even as he expresses some anxiety about having to live with them. He never gives a sustained theoretical treatment of what might throw a polity off a well-planned course, but he does invoke repeatedly the idea that unforeseen events inevitably threaten political societies and can come in a variety of forms. Some events are internal to polities themselves and related to what Locke acknowledges as the "uncertainty and variableness of humane affairs" (*ST,* 156). This category encompasses a number of possibilities enumerated in the *Second Treatise*—ranging from simple social mobility and shifts in the distribution of wealth and property to darker instances of "humane frailty," including unexpected scrambles for dominion and sustained efforts to defraud the public, as his later engagements with political tyranny and a looming coinage crisis document (*ST,* 143, 164, and 225).[6]

Locke also notes the recurrence of unanticipated events that are largely exogenous to the realm of social or political affairs. Among these are accidents, such as natural or even manmade disasters. These events are especially significant for his thought because they draw into focus the limited ability of a standing body of law to address the truly unexpected. Locke suggests that to follow the law rigidly in all cases, even and especially in those that are matters of accident, may bring more harm than benefit to the public. There are, he notes, "many things . . . which the Law can by no means provide for" (*ST,* 159). Legislative bodies cannot always act quickly enough in response to these events, and more to the point, it is simply "impossible to foresee . . . all Accidents and Necessities" that might involve the public (*ST,* 160). The law can never, he reflects, encompass the range of contingencies the future holds, or move as quickly as a public in crisis might need in the aftermath of accident.

As I argue in the next section, Locke is not an opponent of the rule of law, despite his reflections on its limitations. Indeed, he often confronts crises by calling on the law and advocating punishment for those who pose a threat to the public, as we will see in his treatment of the coinage crisis. But, unlike Hobbes, he does not actively resist the perpetual dynamism of the political world and the human inability to know the future, and he is thus skeptical about our ability to prepare for it fully. This position makes strict legalism impossible for Locke.[7] Custom, law, and the rules of political representation are, on some occasions, too rigid or slow to accommodate the strain put upon them by social flux and to promote what Locke takes to be the guiding principle of political life—the pursuit of the common interest.

Locke's unwillingness to look away from the imperfect underlying conditions and deep uncertainty of political life thus leads him to endorse an account of political arrangements and action that is fundamentally open ended (and hence demanding of constant vigilance). For political actors of all stripes, Locke demands a productive if difficult engagement with uncertainty. His acceptance and negotiation of epistemological uncertainty and political contingency generate power in more than one locus, and as I argue in the next section, his depiction of government as a trusteeship facilitates this production and distribution of power.

Lockean Trust: Uncertainty, Judgment, Risk

Locke explicitly models the relationship of a political community to all branches of its government on the idea of a legal fiduciary trust, an arrangement in which someone is declared an owner of property as long as he or she uses that property to benefit another designated person. Locke's theory of relations between rulers and their subjects does not, however, amount to a detailed or rigid legal agreement between trustees and beneficiaries. Rather, he applies the concept of a legal trust as a guiding metaphor for or analogy to state power, which allows him to argue that while rulers "own" their power, they must use it to benefit the ruled and can be held accountable for how they do so. In this chapter, I emphasize that the most important use of this power is for the protection of the public good against anticipated and unanticipated threats. That is, trustee power exists to help a people confront both calculated risks and wholly contingent events, and it can be judged on how ably it works toward this end.

A trust is importantly different in character from another set of political relations in the Lockean polity—those internal to political society. Locke memorably posits that individuals form and sustain a political community by means of a compact, and he therefore conceives of the horizontal networks that structure a political society as ones of mutual obligation and benefit.[8] What is important to keep in mind is that the vertical bond of fiduciary trust between a political society and government does *not* imply this kind of mutuality; the trust exists, at least in theory, only for the benefit of members of political society. We can imagine how rulers might benefit directly from the arrangement, especially those members of the political society who also serve as legislators, but this possibility is not made explicit by the model Locke employs. Theorizing governmental power as trusteeship emphasizes something else instead: that rulers are primarily the bearers of obligation in this scenario, and this obligation is to act always for the public good. The details of this obligation are left unspecified. Trustees are not required, for example, to work with the beneficiaries of the trust to determine the specifics of how rulers might secure the public good; it is entirely up to the government, and not the people, to determine how best to proceed.[9] This task requires trustees to exercise judgment, and it demands a counterbalancing judgment from beneficiaries, who must determine whether the spirit of the trust is being honored.

Locke's reliance on the trust metaphor hardly made him unusual in the context of seventeenth-century British political writing, as supporters of royal and parliamentary rule alike couched accounts of political power in the language of legal trust.[10] Notwithstanding its apparent ordinariness, Lockean trust poses interpretive difficulties. Notably, some scholars resist the possibility that the fiduciary trust analogy does much substantive work for Locke. Peter Laslett, for example, argues that Locke only means to employ "suggestive use of legal language" in his references to a fiduciary trust in the *Second Treatise*. Laslett is also, therefore, unwilling to assume that Locke further intends his readers to view rebellion as a power wielded by defrauded beneficiaries who have judged their trust to be violated.[11] John Dunn, too, is difficult to interpret on this question. He argues that the metaphor "carries little or no distinctive weight in [Locke's] argument," even as he admits that it captures nicely the responsibility of rulers and the psychological burden trust foists on beneficiaries.[12] Against these interpretations, I argue that the formal trust arrangement is unambiguously *the* central device of Locke's political theory, especially if we read him as an early theorist of uncertainty and risk as core problems for political life, as I think we should. This way of figuring political relations effectively reduces the diffuse uncertainty Locke sees as endemic to politics, even as it highlights the inherent risks of living with political authority, a point he wishes to underscore. Trust, as Locke uses it, captures a formal political arrangement, but it also ultimately suggests how political authority might register in the thoughts and emotions of its citizens—as full of promise and peril, profit and loss.[13] That is, Lockean trust frames political authority as a risk, too.

The forms of political action that best illustrate the dual nature of Lockean trust as also a risk are prerogative and popular resistance, opposing modes of exercising political power and judgment, which are held in tension throughout the final chapters of the *Second Treatise*. Whenever governments act as trustees within, outside, or against the law, or citizens resist on the premise that trust has been broken, they are effectively taking a calculated risk, one that might bring them immense political profit or that might make them profoundly worse off. Theorizing the trust model as constituted by risk, as I think Locke does, offers an alternative claim about what stabilizes political societies in practice. Even though Locke says early in the *Second Treatise* that the compact made in nature is what gives polities form and perhaps even longevity, the last and most violent chapters of the *Second Treatise* suggest otherwise. By urging citizen bodies to be perpetually vigilant collectives in his reflections on tyranny and revolution, Locke suggests that, in fact, the common burden and blessing of their status as beneficiaries of a trust continually bind individuals into a political community in the most important way. In the next two sections of this chapter, I analyze the vexing problem of Lockean prerogative and its counterpart, popular resistance, to support this claim.

Trust and the Case of Prerogative Power

By conceptualizing relations of rule as founded on a trust, Locke invites his readers to consider what it could mean practically and psychologically to be subject to extreme political power that need not consult them. Whereas the structure of Locke's polity is quite different from Hobbes's, on this point they bear something of a resemblance. Regardless of whether the exercise of political power turns out to be, in Locke's terms, arbitrary or not, political trust, as Locke formulates it, clearly must entail a willingness to risk the public good in order to protect it. This is most obvious in the case of the exercise of prerogative, a political event in which a trustee's power moves almost wholly unchecked. Lockean citizens must proceed as though their trustees are trustworthy bearers of this power, but with a view to corrective action when they find them not to be.

In light of Locke's apparent commitment to the rule of law and his documented resistance to absolute monarchy, his incorporation of prerogative as a feature of his political theory is deeply unsettling on two counts. First, Locke appears to understand prerogative as wholly extralegal. Second, for him it is a singular power that in practice is most often concentrated in the hands of an executive. Locke's account of prerogative thus suggests that the executive is likely to play an extraordinary role in securing and stabilizing the common interest, and that it may operate outside the law.[14] More strongly, Locke's discussion of prerogative suggests that it frequently *must* do so because of law's limits. Law turns out, Locke notes, to be a partial solution to the challenges a political society faces when trying to achieve common political ends, because it occasionally lacks the ability to accommodate unexpected and urgent problems. By arguing for the necessity of a broad and extralegal prerogative power, Locke weakens the rule of law's force, even as he seeks to accommodate its deficiencies. This is perhaps one of the deepest ironies of Locke's political theory: prerogative is personal discretionary power meant to correct the deficiencies of the rule of law, which was designed to check personal discretionary power in the first place.[15] Here the nature of prerogative power looks something like the nature of risk. Prerogative holds the potential for great political benefit or profit for a community, but this possibility cannot be separated from the kinds of extreme losses it simultaneously threatens.

Given its character, Locke must launch a rigorous defense of prerogative. The first point he raises in its favor is a practical one: legislative bodies are frequently numerically unwieldy, and their activity is sporadic. Locke thinks there are good reasons for the latter, and he in fact recommends that representatives meet to legislate and then adjourn to return to their lives as law-abiding citizens. This way of doing things is convenient, but more importantly, Locke thinks it is hostile to power grabbing on the part of legislators.[16] Unfortunately, this arrangement occasionally stymies timely action. In the case of unforeseen events or accidents, taking the time to convene an assembly and working to reach an agreement in favor of a necessary new law or set of laws is obviously not the best way to mitigate the immediate effects of an unexpected disaster or crisis. If timing is sometimes everything, then responses like these are best left to a standing power—in this case, one already charged with and accustomed to holding perpetual responsibility, such as for the execution of the law.

Locke's concern for timely political action illuminates a related problem with the rule of law that runs deeper and is traceable to his fundamental views on uncertainty and the problem of knowledge. The size and meeting patterns of legislative bodies do not necessarily undermine the rule of law—after all, different political communities can design legislative practices differently, according to need and custom. What will always be true, however, is that legislators lack the foresight or predictive abilities to generate laws that take into account all possible situations that might

characterize the political future. Locke notes in the chapter on prerogative that legislators cannot "foresee, and provide, by Laws, for all, that may
be useful to the Community," and that they most certainly cannot predict
what accidents might befall it, much less legislate with these possibilities
in mind (*ST,* 159–60). Legislators might take into account many contingencies based on experience and knowledge of the past, but their efforts
are ultimately constrained by the cognitive shortcomings that impede all
humans. Although legislators might sometimes impose laws after the fact
to address an unexpected development, some political challenges or crises require immediate action, and these are hard to know in advance.

Locke's concerns about uncertainty and the future lead him to entertain the necessity and usefulness of extralegal power, and prerogative's
extralegal dimension is apparent in how he defines it from the beginning.
According to the earliest definition in the *Second Treatise, prerogative* is

> nothing, but a Power in the hands of the Prince to provide for the
> publick good, in such Cases, which depending on *unforeseen and un-
> certain* Occurrences, certain and unalterable Laws could not safely
> direct, whatsoever shall be done manifestly for the good of the
> People, and the establishing the Government upon its true Foun-
> dations is and always will be just *Prerogative.* (*ST,* 158)

In subsequent definitions—and Locke offers quite a few—he tries to place
some constraints on prerogative. He persistently emphasizes the relationship of prerogative to the public good: it may be exercised only for
the common interest, and not for any other interest or good.[17] Moreover,
he clarifies that although prerogative most often falls with the executive
in practice, it is significantly *not* a constitutive part of executive power.[18]
But when Locke specifies its relation to standing law, he lifts constraints.
The executive who bears prerogative may act when the law is silent and
offers no guidance, but it may also act *against* the legal code "wherein a
strict and rigid Observation of the Laws may do harm" (*ST,* 158). In the
end only one norm really restricts prerogative in practice: *salus populi,* or
the well-being of the public. It follows that acts of prerogative power may
be evaluated only by that most important, and most difficult to define,
standard.

The particular but common case of an executive wielding prerogative
power illustrates starkly how one sided the decision-making aspects of
trusteeship are. Executives may use judgment and skill to do what they like
outside of law in the interest of the people, for holders of prerogative may

decide what to do "of their own free choice" for the public good (*ST,* 164). They are under no obligation to consult with the people regarding which strategies or tactics they ought to employ. The undemocratic character of a trust gives an executive with prerogative great leeway to achieve whatever end is in question, a wide berth that Locke's views on contingency, uncertainty, and prerogative suggest its holder must have. Locke notes that in the case of a good trustee, this is all for the best. A good trustee cannot have "too much *Prerogative*," which he equates here with "Power to do Good" (*ST,* 164). But in problematic or ambiguous cases, the questions of just how bounded prerogative is, and who or what is in place to enforce its limits, become critical. From the beginning, prerogative poses a risk in the dual sense—it can profit the political community, or it can potentially undo it.

What resources are in place to cope with the downsides of prerogative, then? In cases of prerogative gone either too far or terribly awry, Locke argues that the people themselves are the constraint, and that they may operate as one in two ways. First, subjects may redefine the scope of prerogative by pushing for changes in positive law. Locke contends that the people do not encroach on prerogative when they work to limit it by law, and that

> in so doing, they have not pulled from the Prince anything that *of right* belonged to him, but only declared, that that Power, which they indefinitely left in his, or his Ancestors', hands, to be exercised for their good, was not a thing, which they intended him, *when he used it otherwise. (ST,* 163; emphasis added)

Here it becomes important that prerogative is not an executive *right* but is granted to the executive as a power. Thus the people and the legislators who represent their interests may rightly curb its scope by law. This solution may come too late, however, as this kind of legal restriction can only be implemented post hoc. Locke's use of the past tense in this passage implies that people have to experience and suffer the ill use of prerogative first and then may work to limit it, an idea that reemerges in his account of rebellion, the second and more significant way in which the people may limit prerogative, and the focus of this chapter's next section.

I would emphasize here that Locke does not give his readers a very detailed account of the scope and limits of prerogative, and I think he really cannot, at least not by the terms of his own argument for it. His case for incorporating prerogative as a feature of a trust model of government is grounded too deeply in the notion that the unwanted surprises of politics require flexibility. His commitment to this idea necessarily prevents him from specifying or restricting the reach and tactics of the bearer of prerogative power. To put it more bluntly, formally constraining the flexibility of a power meant to cope with flux and the unexpected would render that power superfluous.[19] Thus, Locke leaves citizens to live with the risks of this power.

In the last few chapters of the *Second Treatise*, Locke thus develops the claim that a standing body of law cannot accommodate all that political life entails, and that perhaps what is most essential to the preservation of a common good is knowledge of how and when to act politically. The case of prerogative is one illustration of this idea. Locke leaves unspecified how the holder of prerogative performs the role of guardian of the public good but emphasizes that this responsibility requires skill, judgment, and a keen sense of timing. If used well, prerogative power need not be checked and will simply reinforce trust between subjects and their government. There is ample evidence to suggest, however, that Locke anticipates that executives might very well abuse prerogative, and that prerogative might perpetually overtax rather than shore up trust between a people and its government.[20] In the final chapter of the *Second Treatise*, on popular resistance, Locke considers this possibility in detail, revealing that he is all too aware of the persistent and constitutive risks of trust. This chapter also offers a more full account of what trust is by depicting the trauma of trust broken, when the calculated political risks of an unknown future become harms felt in the present.

Knowing and Rebelling: Popular Power in the Second Treatise

Locke's exploration of why and when political orders may be dissolved and begun anew emphasizes that when people form a political trust, they invite a new risk into their lives: the risk of political authority. Here we see a turn away from the Hobbesian impulse to govern uncertainty out of the world of politics. Locke accepts uncertainty and begins thinking through how many calculable risks political subjects must take. When he comments that the impetus to rebel, "in the change, weakness, and accidents of humane affairs, seldom delays long to offer itself," he seems worried about how often subjects will have to confront grievous political losses aggressively and head on (*ST,* 224). Locke's choice to endorse prerogative may actually speed this process of recognizing loss and resisting it, as revolution is, along with common law, the only check on prerogative power.[21] Locke's work on revolution reveals something important: bound by the relational structure of a public trust, the people carry much the same burden as the holder of prerogative—to act outside of law in service of the common good. The significant difference here is that they bear this responsibility for themselves and not as trustees for others.

The question of how easy or difficult it is for the people to surmise when trust has been destroyed is an open and challenging one, and Locke's arguments for rebellion provide a spectrum of answers. He notes that a people may resist political authority in any number of instances, many of which he details in the *Second Treatise*, despite his effort "not to multiply Cases" (*ST*, 239). The multiple scenarios Locke describes and imagines, however, capture a shared feature of prerogative and resistance—subjects must decide when to rebel on a case-by-case basis, and not even a theory as principled and comprehensive as Locke's can tell them precisely when and on what grounds political power has turned arbitrary and deserves to be unseated. There is no law to apply here, just as the law sometimes fails the holders of prerogative when facing an accident or unexpected crisis that threatens the integrity of the commonwealth. In fact, the only norm that holds here is *salus populi suprema lex*, just as with the exercise of prerogative.

Since the decision to rebel is rooted in judgment and knowledge, it is important to specify the kinds of knowledge revolutionary subjects must possess and how they can acquire it. The question here is not exactly a consideration of whether or how Lockean subjects are able to justify revolutionary acts on the moral grounds elaborated in the *Second Treatise*'s normative account of rights and duties under law. Rather, it is a pragmatic inquiry of sorts—a consideration of whether and how they *know* when the time for revolution is upon them. To a degree, this requires disaggregating the normative and empirical knowledge that revolutionary actors often use in tandem—that is, distinguishing their knowledge that certain kinds of force are unlawful from their concrete experiences or anticipation of injury at the hands of force. Locke himself does not draw these normative and empirical distinctions so clearly in the text, for he expects people will hold and use both kinds of knowledge simultaneously.

While Locke expects variation among cases of revolution, at bottom he argues that knowing when to resist is normally a matter of ascertaining with as much certainty as possible that rule is tyrannical and that the appropriate bounds of authority have been transgressed. In rare but

CHAPTER THREE

critical cases, I argue, the turn to resistance is also a matter of *predicting* the onset of tyranny. This second case is especially important for a study of risk, because it is where probability enters the political picture, and probabilistic reasoning becomes crucial to the most high-stakes exercises of political judgment.

Locke thus argues for two general circumstances in which a populace may resist political authority. First, the people may resist based on the knowledge that they are already well under the thumb of tyranny. This, by and large, assumes a mostly passive public that can easily recognize the obviously destructive choices of a trustee. Much of Locke's work in the *Second Treatise* suggests that this type of case is the norm, such as when he notes that the question of the distinction between prerogative and tyranny will be easily decided by "the good or hurt of the People" (*ST*, 161).[22] The essential point here is that Locke expects that tyranny will be quite obvious to political subjects living with it much of the time. I argue that this does not mean the Lockean public is unsophisticated in its ability to acquire political knowledge of tyranny; it simply suggests that in many cases, this knowledge will not be hard to come by.

Locke spins out the case for tyranny's frequent obviousness in response to a strong objection to his argument that people can legitimately resist political authority. The objection, which Locke himself introduces, is rooted in a charge against the people, that they are ignorant, malcontent, and fickle, and hence liable to overthrow any government that does not sit well with them, whether they are justified in doing so or not. Locke counters the suggestion that he is inciting an already volatile public with a depiction of it as quite slow moving and resistant to change. As he argues, even when political communities do try to enact radical transformations, they often find themselves wandering back to their old forms out of force of habit and in search of comfort (*ST*, 223). The people are, he argues, fundamentally risk averse when it comes to tampering with their current political arrangements.

If Locke is right, then allowing the people to determine when to act against corrupt rule is unlikely to open the door to political chaos. Locke insists that

> such *Revolutions happen* not upon every little mismanagement in publick affairs. *Great mistakes* in the ruling part, many wrong and inconvenient Laws, and all the *slips* of humane frailty will be *born by the People*, without mutiny or murmur. But if a long train of Abuses, Prevarications, and Artifices, all tending the same way, make the

design visible to the People, and they cannot but feel, what they lie under, and see, whither they are going; 'tis not to be wonder'd, that they should then rouze themselves, and endeavour to put the rule into such hands, which may secure to them the ends for which Government was at first erected. (*ST,* 225)

This passage is notable not only for Locke's insistence that it takes a great many missteps to foment revolution, but also for two other pieces of information it yields about how people might know when to resist. First, it suggests that subjects will need to sense their way to revolutionary action. Locke claims that tyranny will be rendered apparent to the people over time by their own basic capacities for feeling and sight, and that abuse makes the design of tyranny visible both by weighing heavily atop them and by pushing them in an undesirable direction, presumably further in harm's way.[23] But still more radically, Locke implies here that people need to know not merely when they are under tyrannical rule, but when they are *going* to be under it. This suggests that revolutionary subjects will sometimes need to think predictively to see beyond where they are to "whither they are going." Unfortunately, Locke makes plain in this passage that the people do not possess the power of foresight, so the design of tyrants, he argues, has to be visible, knowable by the senses.

This is not to say that Locke thinks revolution is justifiable *solely* on the basis of what hurt subjects feel or see. Rather, he understands that the improper use of power is *often* recognized directly through sense and experience. Moreover, it is recognized with certainty, for as he asserts in the *Essay Concerning Human Understanding,* "no body can, in earnest, be so sceptical, as to be uncertain of the Existence of those Things which he sees and feels" (*HU,* 4.11.3). In the subsequent depiction of the near certitude of sensory knowledge that follows this claim, Locke twice gives the example of being burned by fire to make the point that we can know with certainty what fire is when we touch it and hurt ourselves (*HU,* 4.11.7– 8). Our senses grant us certainty enough for our own purposes; while they do not yield "a perfect, clear, comprehensive Knowledge of things free from all doubt and scruple," senses serve well "enough but to the preservation of us, in whom they are; and accommodated to the use of Life" (*HU,* 4.11.8). To return to the example of fire, when we burn ourselves, we may not suddenly comprehend the relationship between fire and oxidation. We can, however, comprehend with enough certainty that fire has a capacity for heat, as well as how this heat could be put to good use and, more importantly for our purposes, how much damage the fire could cause.[24]

Locke thus privileges what we might call sensory knowledge, and the famous passage from the *Second Treatise* about long trains of abuses suggests that he privileges sensory knowledge jointly with past experience as a reliable source of political knowledge. In the last few chapters of the *Second Treatise*, we find a variety of cases in which people experience injury to what law demarcates as their own—their bodies, their labor, their property, and perhaps even their beliefs—and these experiences amount to feeling the effects of tyranny. Such feelings should trigger the obvious realizations that it is time to use force against a tyrant, and that doing so is normatively permissible. If experience is the test of government, then the felt experience of oppression over time is the surest way to know when trustees are no longer trustworthy.[25] The people can thus know when the time has come to resist government, because they feel it so sharply.

While felt experiences of harm are knowable, how are these experiences interpreted further as signs of tyrannical abuses of power? Locke points out that "where-ever Law ends, Tyranny begins," which suggests that subjects' certain experiences of injury to their bodies or property can only be *understood* as tyranny where there is no law. Another possibility is that subjects may also feel and see that the laws and constitutional arrangements that mark out what is theirs are also being subjected to injury (*ST*, 202). This implies that subjects must have, in addition to sensory and experiential knowledge, a firm sense of what legality is as a point of reference when they are making claims about the existence of tyranny as unlawful, arbitrary power.[26]

Another potential stumbling block is that Locke presents tyranny as a political harm experienced by a community, and therefore tyranny has to be named collectively.[27] But he does not demarcate a threshold for when this becomes clear, nor does he elucidate when it is fair for the members of a body politic to surmise that they are experiencing not merely a scattering of individual harms but instead the full force of collective injury. People have to know, for instance, whether the harms befalling a few individuals are actually injuries that threaten the integrity of the commonwealth. How they work this out is not clear from the *Second Treatise*, which does not provide us with the sociology of knowledge we might wish for when it comes to the decision to resist authority. Even when tyranny is obviously and passively detected through the senses, there is still interpretive work to be done with the acquired information, and Locke leaves it to the people to interpret and judge their condition, with their own vision of a desirable future in mind—a vision that may vary from person to person within the community. Locke's work has a difficult opacity with respect to the question of how this process goes, but in spite of this, I argue that what holds a Lockean people together is the collective exercise of this kind of judgment and deliberation.[28]

The even more difficult cases for Lockean subjects, however, are those in which tyranny must be anticipated, and this is where probability and risk enter Locke's considerations of resistance. While Locke recommends sensory and experiential knowledge for their certain character, he notes that they do not solve the critical political problem of timing, the very same problem that animated his endorsement of prerogative power as a political necessity. In chapter 19 of the *Second Treatise*, Locke mounts a claim for *preemptive* revolution as a right. He asserts that

> the state of Mankind is not so miserable that they are not capable of using this remedy till it be too late to look for any . . . Men can never be secure from Tyranny, if there be no means to escape it, till they are perfectly under it: And therefore it is, that they have not only a Right to get out of it *but to prevent it.* (*ST,* 220; emphasis added)

For the people and their good to be secure, they do not need to wait until the burden of abuse becomes so obvious that it is too heavy for them to bear. Put another way, they need not wait until their sensory experiences of tyranny overwhelm them or incapacitate them. Rather, Locke urges them to judge when trust is violated before their bodies and property are seized or crushed and before their institutional arrangements lose all integrity.

This second case for popular rebellion that Locke posits—one that involves anticipatory resistance—is far less common and far more cognitively demanding, but arguably even more urgent. Subjects may resist corrupt authority preemptively, to avoid subjecting themselves or their political forms to potential or burgeoning tyranny. Locke especially emphasizes the importance of anticipatory pushback when the legislative power is starting to come under duress. Subjects must intervene before the legislative body crumbles (and takes with it the executive), for as Locke makes explicit, a political society cannot lose its "Native and Original right . . . to preserve itself, which can *only* be done by a settled Legislative, and a fair and impartial execution of the Laws made by it." If the government is dissolved before the people can intervene and do it themselves, civil society is unlikely to survive, either. By the time its legislative body is gone, then, with respect to its preservation and good, it is "too late, and the evil is past cure" (*ST,* 220). Lockean subjects thus not only must know how straightforward abuses of power feel or look but also must be able to identify more subtle *endeavors* to abuse power. These may take the form of concealed abuses, failed efforts to abuse subjects, or even pathological forms of neglect. Trust can be broken in a number of ways, many of them not terribly obvious. By advocating preemptive revolution, Locke suggests that the beneficiaries of a trust must struggle against passivity and be vigilant, forward thinking, and calculative.[29]

Locke's consideration of preemptive revolution is not the first time in the *Second Treatise* we find him stressing the ways in which timing, prediction, and anticipation are important for the preservation of life and liberty. In chapter 3, "Of the State of War," Locke asserts that it is "lawful" for a man to kill a thief who has neither hurt him nor declared any intention to hurt him beyond robbing him of goods, in part because there is no surefire way of knowing if the theft of goods may eventually give way to something worse. In this case, he affirms that the victim has "a liberty to kill the aggressor, because the aggressor allows not time to appeal to our common Judge, nor the decision of the Law" (*ST,* 19). Law is meant to address claims of injury in light of evidence *after* the alleged moment of force passes, but it does little good in the present moment when one is uncertain about what the outcome of a violent encounter will be. There is time enough for speculation in such situations, Locke thinks, but not for the appeal to law.

In the *Second Treatise*'s chapter on tyranny, Locke again suggests that it is only legitimate to meet force with force when an appeal to law is made impossible. He illustrates this point with contrasting examples of highway robbery. In one case, a man demands the purse of another at sword point. Locke argues that the victim may kill the robber, even if he has not twelve pence in his pocket to hand over to him.[30] In a second scenario, one man asks another to hold his money for a moment, and when he turns to retrieve it, he is then held at sword point and denied what is rightfully his. In this situation, he may *not* lawfully kill the man who robs him. Locke argues that the difference between the two cases is plain. In the former scenario, the victim may kill his robber because the thief uses force to threaten his life, and there is no "time to appeal to the Law to secure it." In the second case, the victim may appeal to the law for reparation once he finds out his money shall not be returned easily. He has time and a range of options for recovering his money, and his life is under no apparent threat (*ST,* 207).

These examples are relevant for the case of anticipatory revolution because they call attention to Locke's insistence that in particular cases, preemptive action rather than an appeal made through legal channels is appropriate. The recommendation of a quick and violent response not to past or even present harms, but to apparent future harms, reflects again Locke's views about timing and choice. Humans are free to exercise judgment to decide whether to use force, if the harms anticipated seem to be irreparable ones. With harms that cannot be rectified once committed, time is of the essence, and thus the choice to appeal to law is, Locke argues, unavailable. This is certainly the case in the first theft scenario from the tyranny chapter, and Locke insists that citizens are compelled to take the same approach if they have reason to believe that their government will soon commit the kinds of political and personal injuries that cannot be rectified later by either law or resistance. The people must, he argues, pay attention to their security and think predictively about the future. That is, they must anticipate and manage the risks of politics by drawing on both their capacity for judgment and their right to resist.

Moving from the more personal cases of robbery back to the collective problem of revolution, Locke again emphasizes the necessity of vigilance and anticipation, the hallmarks of risk calculation, in a particularly striking passage from the *Second Treatise*'s chapter on tyranny. There he offers a metaphor to illustrate his point about attention and the visibility of tyrannical designs. He compares a citizen living under rulers who publicly espouse a commitment to the common interest but quietly undermine it by their actions to a passenger on a boat to the slave market of Algiers. About this citizen, Locke asks:

> How can [he] any more hinder himself from being perswaded in his own Mind, which way things are going; or from casting about how to save himself, than he could from believing the Captain of the Ship he was in, was carrying him, and the rest of the Company to *Algiers,* when he found him always steering that Course, though cross Winds, Leaks in his Ship, and want of Men and Provisions did often force him to turn his course another way for some time, which he steadily returned to again, as soon as the Wind, Weather, and other Circumstances would let him? (*ST,* 210)

Locke wants his citizens to be vigilant subjects who guard against tyranny, much like the observant passenger en route to Algiers guards against his own enslavement. Although Locke says that the passenger cannot help but be persuaded by what he finds, suggesting a passive approach to the acquisition of evidence of tyranny, the metaphor still suggests that citizens must do some intellectual work. They must be able to discern a pattern of tyranny from perhaps contradictory observations—they have to detect the straight course that emerges from the multidirectional twists and turns of politics, figured here as navigation. Here Locke again suggests that although tyranny is not always immediately visible, subjects must be attuned to the possibility of its existence and must commit to careful observation and judgment.[31]

As these examples imply, the decision to rebel preemptively may thus depend on subjects' ability to calculate risk, to think probabilistically about the likelihood of future harm. Subjects must ask whether or not tyranny is the *probable* end of the political maneuvering and activity they have observed and must be able to offer an affirmative answer. This is, unsurprisingly, a difficult task.[32] In *Of the Conduct of the Understanding*, Locke importantly emphasizes the burden that probabilistic reasoning places on individuals. It is, he argues, a matter of examining "all the arguments" pertaining to a particular question "in balance against one another" before determining the outcome. He thinks this is something that can elude even the learned, who are normally trained to look at only two sides to every question. In the political case posed by the *Second Treatise*, most are trained to ask whether tyranny exists or does not. But Locke thinks that early training in probabilistic reasoning for those who—"by the industry and parts of their ancestors have been set free from a constant drudgery to their backs and their bellies"—have the time should produce a more thorough and sophisticated way of addressing questions to which the answer is not easily made out by a single demonstration.[33] For the purposes of this discussion on anticipatory revolution, this kind of training should encourage people to face up to the risk of tyranny and help them learn to reason as ably as they can in the face of uncertain or contradictory evidence. Even in the absence of looming threat, education in probabilistic reasoning and knowledge can only promote the kind of vigilant posture and scrutiny Locke thinks a political trust requires.

Locke's attention to probable thought in his epistemological writings suggests that subjects do have intellectual resources to aid them in their efforts to stop tyranny before they are certain of its existence and, more importantly, before it becomes widespread enough to destroy an entire political society. Probable knowledge is not the surest or most robust form of knowledge, but it is crucial for the survival of political communities.

Despite the attention I have given anticipatory revolution, because of its relation to probabilistic thinking and risk, the *Second Treatise* suggests overwhelmingly that preemptive political violence will be a rare move by the people. While Locke urges vigilance, he admits with some disappointment that "till the mischief be grown general, and the ill designs of the Rulers become visible, or their attempts sensible to the greater part, the People, who are more disposed to suffer than right themselves by Resistance, are not apt to stir" (*ST*, 230). Individuals have trouble thinking beyond what they sense in the immediate moment. Locke describes their difficulty in detail here and elsewhere in the *Treatise*, but still hopes for a vigilant and calculative public attuned to timely political action. As Joshua Dienstag puts it, Locke urges citizens to ask of their political conditions, "What *time* is it?"[34] They must, even in times of relative quiet, be prepared to confront the question of whether the time for revolution is approaching, and they can only rely on judgment to choose well.

Locke's emphasis on timely resistance to an as-yet-unrealized harm at the hands of a tyrannical ruler suggests that Lockean subjects are held together not only by a common set of institutions and moral commitments but also by their constant practices of vigilance and surveillance. Locke's choice to structure political life as a fiduciary trust turns his citizens' gazes away from each other and toward a centralized power. We learn very little about the struggles among individuals that surely characterize political societies after the compact is formed; these interpersonal relationships seem to drop out of Locke's formulation of politics. Instead, our attention is increasingly focused on the anxious relations between a seemingly unified, vigilant people and their government.[35] Although Locke frequently characterizes subjects as prone to noticing only the politically obvious, he still calls for them to be thoughtful and calculative consumers of evidence and producers of political knowledge, because they must be prepared to act at the right time for the preservation of their own good, armed with strong probable belief if not certainty. Such is the burden of being the beneficiary of a trust.

It is important to acknowledge, however, that the standpoint Locke presses on his readers may not issue in perpetual distrust or enmity between them and their rulers but could very well renew belief in the legitimacy of government. In spite of the proliferation of negative examples that characterize the end of the *Second Treatise*, citizenly vigilance and attention to risk may enrich and secure the trust. As we find in a passage in the *Second Treatise*'s chapter on tyranny, if rulers really mean to preserve a people, its good, and its laws and constitution, a political trusteeship will make it so that they cannot help but "see and feel" their trustee's care (*ST,* 209). The posture Locke urges his readers to adopt may, therefore, strengthen the bond between rulers and ruled, as scrutiny yields constant evidence that the spirit of the trust is being honored rather than violated, and as rulers understand that they must work to make their intentions clear.

Trust, Knowledge, and Political Agency

To recapitulate the argument of this chapter, I claim that Locke's political theory distills two important features of trust or qualities of trusting relationships that are not always readily apparent. First, his account of political authority as a trusteeship emphasizes that trusting relationships are often characterized by power asymmetries, or at least by shifting, somewhat unstable power relations. Because Locke's work focuses on the perpetual activity of entrusting—in this case, the people entrust their good to government—it draws into focus the often-lopsided power dynamic of a trust. In particular, Locke's insistence that prerogative is a necessary tool for trustees makes evident the extreme vulnerability of those doing the entrusting and deemphasizes the ways in which trust can be mutual, a kind of partnership between equals. While trust is, Locke argues, the best way to cope with uncertainty, it brings with it a slew of attendant risks generated by exposure to nearly unchecked power. As such, Locke notices early that the risks of politics are perpetual. Even when we try to manage some of them, we create new ones. His work thus yields the insight that risk is a permanent condition of modern life.

Locke's work also offers a rather poignant answer to the question of how people can know what trust is, or what it means. His argument for the legitimacy and necessity of revolution takes up the problem of when individuals and collectives know they should resist. This is, in effect, an inquiry into how people know when trust is violated. That Locke ends his account of the generation and sustenance of polities with reflections on the breakdown of trust, and dedicates more intellectual energy to this than to considerations of how trust is built or sustained, suggests that we often know best what trust is retroactively. That is, we are able to understand the substance of trust, and the kinds of obligations, bonds, and security it entails, in those moments when it is destroyed. We know trust better by feeling its absence or violation, perhaps, than we do when it quietly does its work. Locke's account of revolution reflects the point of view of those who entrust their well-being to others, and his emphasis on the vulnerability and frequent disappointments suffered by those who trust raises questions about what the orientation of the trusting party should be and how attentive that party should be to the problem of risk.

Locke also openly struggles with the problem of when we ought to test the extent and robustness of the trust we have with others, and he investigates what resources people have at their disposal to perform such tests. Locke argues forcefully for the idea that political subjects must use all their available intellectual resources whenever they entrust their well-being to power, a choice he affirms as the best way to cope with the flux and uncertainty that characterize political life. By positioning themselves as the potential beneficiaries of a political trust, they reduce blind uncertainty to a risk that can become an object of knowledge—subjects can observe and scrutinize those who rule them to ensure that rulers continue to deserve their trust. One could object, perhaps rightly, that Locke's emphasis on the perpetual cognitive work that trusting requires suggests that Lockean subjects are, in fact, quite distrustful. I would argue, however, that this is not really Locke's central point about trust. Rather, his work encourages a heightened awareness of how risk and trust are always intertwined, and moreover, this insight yields a useful and unusual account of political agency that is not *only* focused on action or the exercise of freedom or power, although it is partly. While Locke attends always to the necessity of action in politics, his account of revolution as provoked by broken trust also relies on a view of political agents as embodied, thinking subjects, who rely on sense and cognition to steer their own courses. The quest for knowledge, however limited and difficult, is an important component of Lockean politics, and one that deeply informs the practice of political trust.

Economy, Uncertainty, and Risk: The Coinage Controversy

I have argued thus far that Locke's theory of politics, when coupled with his epistemology, provides a fruitful but still fairly implicit engagement with the problem of risk as it relates to trust, the cornerstone of Locke's positive theory of political relationships. I end this chapter with a brief consideration of another aspect of Locke's thought, his work on economy. In his writings on money and interest especially, he uses the word "risk" often.[36] For him, the word "risk" is tied intimately to the possibility of commercial loss. Although I have argued that his body of work on knowledge and politics provides a full and quite rich conceptual apparatus for thinking about probability, risk, and trust, the story there is also one of the hazards and potential losses of political life.

Locke's explicit engagement with a narrow rendering of risk as loss in the commercial world intersects with his broader conceptual account of risk and trust when we examine his efforts to solve the commonwealth's coinage crisis in the mid-1690s, a predicament that resulted in the Great Recoinage of 1696. The coinage crisis was the result of the fraudulent practices of tradesmen and bankers, who were disrupting the value and stability of currency by siphoning off silver bullion from the nation's stock of hard currency. They managed to pilfer it in several ways. Some clipped the edges off hand-struck coins, stockpiled and smuggled the silver clippings out into a global currency market, and then tried to use defective light coins for their original value (value understood as quantity or weight in silver). Others forged coins and passed them off as legitimate products of the mint, and still others melted down silver pieces and smuggled them abroad, as the bullion itself was worth more abroad than it was valued in Britain.[37]

This wide-ranging abuse of currency, which enacted a very slow but disturbing drain of bullion from the treasury, had far-reaching consequences beyond its status as flagrant theft.[38] The deeper problem with coin clipping was that "the recognized and generally accepted value of the common currency was being undermined," which for Locke amounted to an epistemological crisis, as "coin-clippers were unsettling the settled and established meaning of money" and thereby breaking the trust that is central to economic exchange.[39] While the coin clippers risked material loss for the commonwealth so that they could speculate in pursuit of short-term gain for themselves, what really troubled Locke was the loss of meaning and the resulting uncertainty for the whole commercial community.[40] This was most certainly an instance of the "humane frailty" he cites as a cause of the difficult flux and unanticipated crises that characterize politics—only here he spotted it in England's nascent commercial society.

Worries about the sudden uncertainty obscuring the value of coin, the risks posed by the instability of money, and the resulting epistemological and material crisis for public trust play out in Locke's *Further Considerations Concerning Raising the Value of Money*. This 1695 document represents Locke's position in the debate about how to confront the (quite literally) damaged state of English currency and the crisis of value and trust it was provoking. In short, Locke argued for recalling the whole lot of damaged coin and reissuing new silver coins at the old weight and standard of value. Beginning anew, he thought, could stabilize what was being threatened by the risky endeavors of bankers and tradesmen bent on private profit—the value of currency, rooted in its weight.[41] Beyond this policy recommendation, however, the document is also interesting for what it has to say about uncertainty, knowledge, and a stable politics of trust. For Locke, silver coin was most important as a measure of value, facilitating trade and interactions among people who agreed on it as a unit of exchange. Throwing the value and meaning of silver into question threatened to put the peaceable character of commerce, and perhaps the unity of the body politic itself, at risk.

Locke defined silver as both the instrument and the measure of commerce "in all the civilized and trading parts of the world" (*FCM*, 410). In terms of measure, the quantity of silver counted, but as an instrument of commerce, silver's value mattered most. This settled value held the commonwealth together along with other forms of agreement and consent:

> The intrinsick value of Silver consider'd as Money, is that estimate which common consent has placed on it, whereby it is made Equivalent to all other things, and consequently is the universal Barter or Exchange which Men give and receive for other things they would purchase or part with for a valuable consideration: And thus as the Wise Man tells us, *Money answers all things*. (*FCM*, 410)

Consent and agreement, that is, trust among trading partners, settled the value of silver, and this trust was at risk when coins were clipped. To honor the agreement among trading partners, the quantity of silver had to be guaranteed in the individual coins. Yet, the quantity was being altered and then misrepresented by coin clippers, undermining the value of silver as a currency in the process.

But clipped coins also altered the character of trade and exchange, as it was frequently the seller who found himself left with less valuable coin than he had bargained for, or who was required to judge and refuse any coin he suspected of being clipped. Locke writes, "'[T]is no wonder if the price and value of things be *confounded and uncertain*, when the measure itself is lost. For we have now no lawful Silver Money current among us: And therefore *cannot talk nor judge right*, by our present uncertain clip'd Money, of the value and price of things" (*FCM*, 430; emphasis added). Exchange and trade are relations of trust that depend on prior agreement on value between partners, who facilitate exchange through communication and good judgment. If exchange partners cannot "talk or judge right," they are left vulnerable. Threatening the value of currency turns these exchanges into risky ventures that require vigilance and even suspicion about the medium of exchange itself. Thus "clipping, and clip'd Money, have besides this robbery of the Publick other great inconveniencies: As the disordering of Trade, raising Foreign Exchange, and a general disturbance which every one feels thereby in his private affairs" (*FCM*, 418). The shocks of coin clipping were felt by the public as a whole and by private men as well, not simply in terms of material loss, but also in terms of deep epistemological uncertainty about the very unit of value that underpinned economic transactions.

For Locke, it was up to the state, as the trustee of the public good, to confront this problem with policy. Though individual economic actors could refuse coins they suspected were clipped, the policy solution to the problem was an endeavor with higher stakes. Locke wanted to preserve the link between quantity and value in the coin, and he fought against propositions and solutions that would parse the two by lowering the weight of coin:

> Clipping of Money is raising it without publick Authority; the same denomination remaining to the piece, that hath now less Silver in it than it had before.
>
> Altering the Standard, by Coining pieces under the same denomination with less Silver in them than they formerly had, is doing the same thing by publick Authority. The only odds is, that by Clipping the loss is not *forced* on any one (for nobody is obliged to receive Clip'd Money;) By altering the Standard it is. (*FCM*, 417)

By Locke's lights, the issue came down to whether the architects of monetary policy wished to preserve the public trust or destroy it by forcing a lower standard of value on economic actors.[42] Possibilities for undermining the public trust abounded—from the individual exchanges that suddenly grew very risky due to the circulation of clipped coins, to the possibility of legislation that would formalize the devaluation of silver, a prospect Locke warned against. In Locke's view, it was up to the state to develop a system that would shield citizens from potential loss at the hands of other commercial actors, as well as at the hands of the state.

Conclusion

Locke won the fight to preserve the old money standard, but the Great Recoinage of 1696 was still disturbing to the commercial economy of England.[43] Locke's arguments about coinage and value, however, are not of interest in this chapter for their correctness or ultimate political expediency. Rather, they serve two other purposes. First, they provide a practical example of the arguments about risk and trust that animate Locke's account of common life. The monetary crisis, provoked by the self-interested activities of fraudulent currency speculators, struck at the foundation of Locke's commonwealth—trust—by generating uncertainty on at least three registers. First, the very terms of exchange were rendered uncertain by the circulation of clipped coins, such that trade became an enterprise risking both material loss and loss of clear knowledge about the terms of engagement and value. Second, the crisis eroded the interpersonal trust that mediated the risk of exchange. If clipping coins and passing them off as standard currency was possible, currency and trading partners both had to be perpetually scrutinized as potential risks to both epistemological and material security, perhaps to the degree that dealing with trading partners was no longer even worth the risk. Finally, the state, as a trustee of the common good, had to restore the value and meaning of currency, in turn securing stability and security for commerce. To give in on this question and meet the low standard set by coin clippers was, for Locke, a violation of the public trust. Thus policy debates were a place to test the robustness and strength of the public trust to combat the disruptive behaviors of coin clippers. Governing the risks of exchange depended not only on controlling wayward profiteers bent on clipping coins, but also on restoring the shared meaning of and public confidence in the coin as a unit of value and exchange, and perhaps in turn the confidence of the people in the state, its trustee.

CHAPTER FOUR

HUME'S FINE BALANCE

On Probability, Fear, and the Risks of Trade

D avid Hume's body of work, with its especially detailed and influential account of probability, is, at first glance, an obvious resource for a story about the rise of risk in early modern Britain.[1] But, as I argue in this chapter, Hume's work has much more to offer students of risk than a theory of probability. He also gives us a vivid depiction of how human beings face uncertainty, as well as advice on the difficult question of how to *live* with risk.

Hume is committed to the view that uncertainty has an important upside. It forces a critical and useful skepticism on human beings, he argues—a view that sets him apart from the earlier thinkers who are central to this book. But, like both Hobbes and Locke, Hume understands how hard it is to live with uncertainty. More importantly, Hume is also exceptionally mindful of how, even if humans can push past the morass of uncertainty to identify probable future outcomes, the anxiety provoked by uncertainty remains untouched. He notes in *A Treatise of Human Nature* that even though uncertainty can trigger hope *and* fear in individuals, in practice, it seems to generate mostly fear and discomfort. And this is true even when people are in possession of relatively secure probable knowledge about the future. Especially in the *Treatise*, Hume presents what is perhaps the most compelling psychological account of the anxieties produced by uncertainty since Hobbes's *Leviathan*, by articulating and describing the apprehensions called forth by thinking about taking risks against a backdrop of uncertainty. Not merely diagnostic, his work offers a corrective to the problem he notices, one offered in his essays on the politics, culture, and economy of commercial societies.

Hume's essays for a general reading public were meant as a therapeutic resource for those who might need or want to shake off the paralysis of uncertainty, at least to a sufficient degree to pursue the kinds of risky ventures that politics and commerce often require. The essay form is particularly suited to mediating skepticism and uncertainty, as Hume explains. An essay's inherently roomy, conversational style invites readers to be part of a process of drawing on disparate experiences to refine and produce provisional knowledge that might serve an active commercial life well. Beyond building a store of useful experiential knowledge in the reader, the essay cultivates relations of trust between essayist and reading public, and perhaps instantiates a community among readers who feel somewhat isolated with their anxieties about the future.

In this chapter I contend that Hume tries to use the essay genre to coax his readers into an attitudinal shift regarding risk taking. In particular, Hume's critique of mercantilism's parochial approach to trade and his arguments for a self-regulating economy, both of which he articulates in his essays, are supposed to recalibrate his readers' sensibilities about the risky aspects of trade. Anticipating that members of a commercial public would fixate on both the probable and improbable *misfortunes*—the bad sides of risk—introduced by complex and increasingly international economic exchanges, Hume introduces the idea of a balanced commercial system in which risk taking ultimately pays off for the whole nation-state, or at least does not hurt individual participants in the political economy quite so badly in the long term. As such, he introduces the case for the other side of risk, in which even daunting economic ventures offer an opportunity for profit and a cause for hope for a better future.

Hume's Experimentalism and the Turn to Probability

For thinking about the problem of risk, one feature of Hume's account of uncertainty and partial knowledge is of particular and lasting importance—his elaborate taxonomy of probability. He formulates his views on probability in *A Treatise of Human Nature* and in *An Enquiry Concerning Human Understanding*, and his work in these two texts sharpens and develops the philosophical account of probability that we find in Locke's epistemological work. This chapter will thus begin by revisiting Hume's contribution to probability theory before turning to his insights on our affective orientations to thinking about the future in terms of risk.

Hume establishes probability as a nonrational mental habit that helps individuals proceed in the face of uncertainty. Hume's account of the limits and possibilities of inductive reasoning, particularly probability, opens into an important insight about risk. He concludes that while humans know full well that probability does not produce incontrovertible knowledge, we think probabilistically anyway by custom and habit. For Hume, then, the ordinary person is already well on his or her way to thinking about the future in terms of risk, largely out of force of habit. Hume thus frames his entire treatment of probabilistic thinking as an ordinary, everyday practice that individuals follow without much prodding.

For Hume, the human tendency to default to probability is a mixed bag, however. It gives actors *some* grounds—often quite convincing grounds—on which to proceed in the face of uncertainty. The usefulness of probabilistic knowledge thus cannot be underestimated; it helps people live in the world. But, Hume acknowledges, even as human beings move almost instantly to probability when confronting the unknown, this cognitive work is still very taxing psychologically. As I argue in this chapter, Hume shows that while human beings *must* act based largely on makeshift accounts of a probable future, the very act of thinking probabilistically transforms us into fearful and risk-averse actors. But before we turn to the debilitating psychological effects of probability and Hume's effort to counter them, a sketch of Hume's taxonomy of probability is in order.

Early in *Treatise*, Hume asserts that any moral science should be built on what he takes to be "the only solid foundation"—one of "experience and observation" (*T,* introduction.7, 4). Following the lead of experimentalists in the natural sciences, Hume's assumption is that the human mind is as unknown to scholars as bodies in the natural world are, so "it must be equally impossible to form any notion of its powers and qualities otherwise than from careful and exact experiments, and the observation of those particular effects, which result from its different circumstances and situations" (*T,* introduction.8, 5). These experiments amount mostly to systematic observations of human experience. That the moral sciences cannot move beyond experience is not a defect for Hume. He is perfectly fine with this reliance on experiments, understood as "experience and observation" of the world, to articulate "matters of fact." Experiments are not only a common feature of the work of natural scientists, but they are also integral to the day-to-day lives of all people.[2] This is simply what everyone does—all people refer to experience or observations to draw inferences about the past, present, and future. Hume thus casts his lot with an experimental approach to human, or moral, sciences, in opposition to more abstract approaches. Significantly, he does so partly *because* of the common quality, or ordinariness, of the method.

Hume acknowledges, however, that the experimental moral sciences are set apart from the natural sciences by a special difficulty. The problem lies with the scientist, in this case. Moral philosophers might be tempted to draw and reflect on their own experiences as part of their experimental method, and this might either alter the social phenomenon they are observing, or taint their observations and how they report them.[3] Hume finds a way around this problem by suggesting that experimental moral philosophy should widen its scope and assemble a *collection* of observations of "human life, [taking] them as they appear in the common course of the world, by men's behavior in company, in affairs, and their pleasures" (*T*, introduction.10, 6). This more social account of knowledge production makes it possible for philosophers to move beyond their own powers of introspection and reflection, which are perhaps too unreliable to stand as authoritative on their own.

By comparing their experiences with those of others, experimental moral philosophers might be able to establish a social science no *less* certain and, Hume hopes, much *more* useful than what is currently on offer. In the *Treatise*, Hume charges that philosophical approaches claiming to be able to uncover "original qualities of human nature" without the use of experiential reasoning are "presumptuous and chimerical" (*T*, introduction.8, 5).[4] In his reflections on the uses of essay writing, the genre that will occasion his important interventions on risk and commerce, Hume again criticizes the kind of philosophy the experimental approach is meant to replace:

> Learning has been as great a Loser by being shut up in Colleges and Cells, and secluded from the World and good Company . . . Even philosophy went to Wrack by this moaping recluse Method of Study, and became as chimerical in her Conclusions as she was unintelligible in her Stile and Manner of Delivery. And indeed, what cou'd be expected from Men who never consulted Experience in any of their Reasonings, or who never search'd for that Experience, where alone it is to be found, in common Life and Conversation? (*EMPL*, 534–35)

Hume insists here that philosophical inquiry, particularly when used in the service of developing a human science, can tell men nothing they might want to know unless it is grounded in lived experience. Moreover, philosophical inquiry of the kind Hume endorses is best done in community with others, so that experiences and observations can be aggregated, shared, and pondered.

Even as he is committed to experimental methods, Hume's skepticism about how *any* person can know "matters of fact" with certainty still pervades his work on epistemology and knowledge—first in the *Treatise*, and then in his later work in the abstract of the *Treatise* and in the *Enquiry Concerning Human Understanding*. The major questions raised by his work on induction from experience as a route to knowledge are ones about the future: How can people know whether what they might experience in the future will be like what they have experienced in the past? How can they plan for the unknown? These are the core questions that underpin how people conceptualize risk and frame decisions to take or to avoid risks in the future, and unsurprisingly, we find them in Hume's treatment of probability.[5]

The most critical tool Hume offers for coping with an unknown future is probability, which he treats with great detail and seriousness, despite his insistence that no one ought to deem it rational. In fact, Hume complains in the abstract to the *Treatise* that his predecessors have spilled too much ink over the study of how human beings produce demonstrable knowledge and have given short shrift to the examination of "probabilities, and those other measures of evidence on which life and action *entirely* depend, and which are our guides even in most of our philosophical speculations" (*T*, abstract.4, 408; emphasis added). Hume goes on to offer his *Treatise* as a corrective to this imbalance, giving what he sees to be extra weight to probability to make up for the deficiencies in the work of his predecessors. This is no small contribution, for as Hume argues, life and action in the face of uncertainty rely entirely on probabilistic knowledge, and we have to live with uncertainty, day in and day out. It is no wonder, then, that Hume parses and describes its forms so carefully.

Hume presents a three-pronged conception of philosophical probability: the probability of chance, the probability of causes, and a third category that he calls "proofs." Beginning with the last of these provides an opportunity to situate Hume's views in the context of what came before his work, at least by his own account. Early in the *Treatise*'s discussion of probability, Hume notes the typical division of knowledge into demonstrable knowledge and probability. Demonstrable knowledge is "that evidence, which arises from the comparison of ideas," exemplified by the knowledge produced by mathematics. All reasoning about cause and effect, grounded in experiential knowledge, is grouped under the broad category of "probability," a decidedly lesser form of knowledge—inferior for its lack of certainty (*T*, 1.3.11.2, 86).[6] This split indicates that even the most painstaking collection of experiential knowledge on a subject will only ever produce knowledge that is *probably* true, and hence neither totally reliable nor perhaps even worthy of assent.

Hume holds this distinction between demonstration and probability steadily, but he interjects a third and significant category of knowledge between them: proof. To define proof, he draws on the common experiences of his readers:

> In common discourse, we readily affirm, that many arguments from causation exceed probability, and may be receiv'd as a superior kind of evidence. One wou'd appear ridiculous who would say, that 'tis only *probable* the sun will rise to-morrow or that all men must dye; tho' 'tis plain we have no farther assurance of these facts than what experience affords us. (*T,* 1.3.11.2, 86; emphasis added)[7]

Hume goes on to say that proofs, while technically fallible and nondemonstrable, are still "entirely free from doubt and uncertainty" (*T,* 1.3.11.2, 86). Elsewhere, he suggests that this is so because they are derived from a store of "uniform experience" that points to underlying laws of nature and thus can be dissolved only by means of an opposing proof (*EHU,* 10.12, 101). So, to use Hume's example, while there always remains the faint possibility that the sun will not rise again tomorrow, it is still quite safe to conjecture that it will. This knowledge of the future, while still wholly experiential, holds the special and secure status of proof. By theorizing proof as a stable category of knowledge, Hume might be giving some reassurance to readers who have to rely on probability at all times, but he also uses proof to emphasize what *mere* probability is: a truly probable argument generates uncertainty that is "real and practical, rather than merely academic[,] as is the case with a proving argument."[8] As will become clear, mere probability is a condition that, Hume argues, has psychological effects and may stymie action. It is better to proceed on proof whenever possible, as proof can also be deployed to counter mere probabilities and to soothe the anxieties raised by uncertainty.

Of Hume's slightly trimmed conception of probability (understood now as arguments from experience about which we are *less* certain), two kinds exist: the probability of chances and the probability of causes. He discusses each at length in the *Treatise*, in brief in the *Enquiry Concerning Human Understanding*, and fleetingly in the opening of his essay on the rise and progress of the arts and sciences, in which he notes with typical self-confidence that it takes a thinker of uncommon subtlety to know the difference between the two.[9]

Hume's account of the probability of chances turns on the following claim: In matters of chance, people can draw on past experiences to infer that *one* of a set of possible outcomes will come to be in the future, but experience does not reveal *which* outcome to expect. To take an example from the *Treatise*, if we cast a six-sided, six-numbered die over and over again, we will come to expect that one of the sides will face upward, but our increasing store of experience will never enable us to discern which of the six sides is more likely to be the one this time. With each toss of the die, we hold no belief that one side will turn up over the others. Put another way, when considering the six sides of the die, we believe equally that each of the six could be the one. As Hume explains, "the original impulse and consequently the vivacity of thought" that issues in favor of one particular outcome is "divided and split in pieces by the intermingled chances" for any one of six outcomes as we repeat the die toss (*T*, 1. 3.11.12, 89).[10] Even with strictly mathematical probabilities, Hume establishes a psychological process of "balancing mental impulses," which mediates between the objective qualities of the game—the features of the die, for example—and the observer's subjective belief in probable outcomes—in this case, the observer's indifference. Hume also considers a second example in which an observer might develop a belief about possible outcomes that is *not* indifferent: if the same six-sided die were marked on four sides with the same figure (say, X), and on two sides with a second, different figure (say, Y), we would expect a stronger possibility that the side of the die that lands face up might show the first figure. That is, the belief that we would throw an X would be stronger than the belief that we would throw a Y.[11]

The second type of probability that Hume theorizes is the probability of causes, which, like the probability of chances, draws on a store of past experiences to inform beliefs about future outcomes. The "probability of causes" category is more like a wide spectrum of probabilities. As Hume explains:

> The probabilities of causes are of several kinds; but are all deriv'd from the same origin, viz. *the association of ideas to a present impression.* As the habit, which produces the association, arises from the frequent conjunction of objects, it must arrive at its perfection by degrees, and must acquire new force from each instance, that falls

under our observation . . .'tis by these slow steps, that our judgment arrives at full assurance. But before it attains this pitch of perfection, it passes thro' several inferior degrees, and in all of them is only to be esteem'd a presumption or probability. The gradation, therefore, from probabilities to proofs is in many cases insensible; and the difference betwixt these kinds of evidence is more easily perceiv'd in the remote degrees, than in the near and contiguous. (*T*, 1.3.12.2, 90)

The claim here is that repeated experiments (or observations of experience) over time can slowly yield greater assurance that expectations for the conformity of future events to past experiments are reasonable, even if, as Hume thinks, these beliefs will never hold the status of knowledge. He also suggests here that people can expect to produce over the courses of their lives a variety of probable belief claims that are more or less certain by degree.

On this spectrum of probable belief claims, the most certain of all are, of course, proofs. In these cases, the formation of beliefs about future outcomes is not especially arduous cognitive work. As Hume describes proofs, "there are some causes, which are entirely uniform and constant in producing a particular effect; and no instance has ever yet been found of any failure or irregularity in their operation" (*EHU*, 6.4, 55). Fire, he explains, has always burned. At this point in human experience, there is no need to observe the burning of many fires over time to draw this conclusion. So in some cases, people can be all but certain about causal probabilities, but not in most cases.

Of the less certain cases, which characterize most of the human experience with probability of causes, Hume posits three varieties: probabilities arising from imperfect experience, probabilities derived from contrary causes, and probabilities by analogy. Probabilities arising from imperfect experience resemble proofs, only they do not rely on constant repetition of experience. Rather, in some cases, they need only rely on one well-conducted experiment or one particularly astute observation of a single experience to make a probable claim about what we might expect in the future. Barry Gower offers a helpful example: "A single well attested observation of the plumage of a new species of bird should establish the color characteristic of the species."[12] In cases like these, Hume notes, we might hesitate to argue for probable belief given that we have made only a single observation, until we recall that many millions of experiments have shown that *"like objects, plac'd in like circumstances, will always produce like effects*; and as this principle has establish'd itself by a sufficient custom, it bestows an evidence and firmness on any opinion, to which it can be apply'd" (*T*, 1.3.8.14, 73).[13] This frees the experimental philosopher from the demands of repetition in some cases. Hume notes that if these kinds of probabilities from insufficient experience are shown to be false, it is not from want of enough experience but rather from the appearance of contrary experiences that falsify current probable claims.

This opens into the second kind of probability of cause—the cases in which diligently performed repeated experiments of careful observation produce contradictory evidence. The existence of contradictory evidence arising during repetition, Hume argues, may be due to contrary causes. To modify slightly Hume's example from the *Treatise*, a pocket watch may run perfectly every day for twenty days, but on the twenty-first day, it may stop—not because its springs are unreliable, but because a speck of sand may have infiltrated the watch and halted its usual and expected routine (*T*, 1.3.12.5, 91). Hume anticipates that people will approach these probabilities much as they approach probabilities of chance. To use another of his examples, an observer documents that of a total of twenty ships that have left port, only nineteen have returned safely. Perhaps the twentieth was stopped by some contingent event, like a storm. If, one day, the observer spots another ship departing, he immediately begins applying his experiential knowledge of past events to determine the chances of the ship's safe return. Because he is working with nineteen concurring experiences and one outlier, he assumes that in this round, the ship is likely to return, but his belief is weakened a little by his past observation of a one-in-twenty likelihood of a ship's disappearance. In Hume's view, "every past experiment may be consider'd as a kind of chance; it being uncertain to us, whether the object will exist conformable to one experiment or another" (*T*, 1.3.12.11, 92). When experiments do not always conform, observers will always be (more or less) uncertain. It turns out that, like probability of chance, this species of probability of causes is quantifiable for Hume. Observers accumulate superior and inferior numbers of chances when they watch the die being thrown repeatedly, and they also sort and tally the frequency of the causes of past experiences in much the same way. Hume suggests that human beings automatically subject observations to a calculus.[14] Probability calculations, while by definition uncertain, can still be rather precise, at least as Hume figures them. This precision does not free people, however, from the creeping anxiety that marks all considerations of an uncertain future, a problem that Hume notices and that will be important for this chapter.

The third species of probability of causes that Hume classifies is probability by analogy. In the cases of probabilities of chances and contrary causes, strength of belief in a future outcome depends on two things: repetition of past events and experiences, and the presence of a new event that resembles past ones, such that we are immediately compelled to compare past and present to predict a future outcome. Probable beliefs are stronger or weaker in the cases of chance and contrary causes depending on how many times experiments issue in the same results. So, when watching a ship depart, we believe more strongly that it will return if we have seen nineteen of twenty ships return safely in the past than if we have observed only fifteen of twenty ships return. In probability by analogy, beliefs are potentially weakened by the imperfect resemblance between a present event and observed past events. In other words, the strength of probable belief varies more or less with the degree of similarity or resemblance between past events and what can be observed now. In *An Enquiry Concerning Human Understanding*, Hume gives an example to illustrate probabilistic reasoning by analogy—conclusions drawn from anatomical studies performed on one animal may be presumed to apply to other animals, such as when one discovers the circulation of blood in a frog and assumes that it circulates in other kinds of animals as well, to greater or lesser degree depending on how closely the species resemble (*EHU*, 9.1, 92).

Thus concludes Hume's taxonomy of philosophical probability. Though he parses it strictly from demonstrable knowledge, he maintains that it rests on "reasonable foundations of belief and opinion" and can be "receiv'd by philosophers" as a respectable approach to reasoning about the future (*T*, 1.3.13.1, 97). This is not where he ends his account of probabilistic reasoning, however; he goes on to think about exceptions to what he has described and theorized.

In the *Treatise*, Hume documents ways in which probability can go awry in practice or can be deemed *un*philosophical. He names four obstacles to philosophical probability, all of which throw off the ability to perform the kind of unconsciously quantitative weighing and measuring that Hume thinks many forms of probable thought require. The first and second of these are temporal obstacles. First, an argument from probability constructed today may have less force in the future, as both the calculations made and the evidence gathered may hold a different weight in a different future. As Hume argues, "Circumstance has a considerable influence on the understanding, and secretly changes the authority of the same argument, according to the different times, in which it is pro- pos'd to us" (*T,* 1.3.13.1, 98). That is to say, social and cultural context matters when it comes to judging the authority of a probabilistic argu- ment. The second challenge also has to do with the passing of time. Ex- periments run most recently are the ones that will influence judgment and the passions most strongly, and we might be tempted to assign them more weight than they warrant. Hume here gives the example of an alco- holic who loses a friend to the disease—he has a heightened view in the short term of the risks he runs by continuing to drink, but over time, his memory of the experience fades, and his fear and caution subside.

The third type of unphilosophical probability has to do with how peo- ple render probable arguments. Hume argues that the more complicated the probable argument, the less force it has. In fact, what might stand as a proof starts to look like mere probability, unless it is presented as di- rectly and as simply as possible. This insight relates to the prior point about the freshness of experience. In this case, experience and its force are dulled when subjected to long argument.

Here Hume pauses for a brief reflection on time and argument, which is also poignant given his own looming future as a famed historian and man of letters. Despite his insistence that the strength of belief rests on both the proximity of experience in time and the simplicity of arguments we make from experience, he notices that we still believe quite strongly in the events and persons of ancient history, which are long past and con- veyed to us through complex modes of transition. How can history still hold force? Hume thinks that trust and fidelity ameliorate the problem of the passage of time—the trustworthiness of "printers and copists" to pre- serve and transcribe exactly and faithfully each edition of a history as it comes their way allows readers to believe with some confidence in the ex- periences and persons that would otherwise have faded entirely from view (*T,* 1.3.13.6, 99).

Returning to the treatment of unphilosophical probability, Hume ex- presses a fourth and final worry about the tendency to form general rules too hastily from probabilities by analogy, which then harden into prej- udices. Hume includes among these national or ethnic prejudices that lead people to inaccurate or offensive judgments. These generalizations are importantly different from the kinds that people make from a long series or even a small number of well-run experiments. In the cases of un- duly formed prejudices, Hume argues, the habitual practice of probabil- ity has not followed its due course.

Why give attention to these four challenges to sound probabilistic thinking, pathologies that might very well combine in various ways to undermine the process by which humans acquire most of their existing knowledge about the natural and social world? After all, Hume has worked hard to detail a complex account of the relationship between the frequency of experience, the process by which observers of that experience measure probability, and the generation of stronger or weaker belief, all while arguing that the process is a matter of habit. By attending to unphilosophical probabilities, Hume underscores the volatility of probabilistic reasoning. While establishing that probability calculation is a common practice and, in many instances, a reliable practice, he still documents all the ways in which greater uncertainty and error can permeate this already uncertain path to reasonable judgments about the future. Recall that the mechanisms by which people generate philosophical probabilities and unphilosophical probabilities are the same. It is up to observers to be vigilant and resist giving way to the latter by weighing evidence as carefully as possible and making claims about the future with as much precision as they can. This is also the work that underpins the experience of living with risk—the careful effort to make the kind of rigorous probabilistic claims about an unknown future that are so useful when people *must* act and wish to do so prudently. Hume's insight is that this work is often difficult and ridden with cognitive pitfalls, even though all people turn to it almost by default.

In addition to Hume's apparent emphasis on the cognitive challenges posed by probabilistic reasoning, he also stresses that doing this kind of thinking and reasoning is emotionally taxing. Hume supplements his rich rendering of how people reason probabilistically with an equally detailed account of how this process registers affectively, with disconcerting findings. Essentially, his claim is that the very process of thinking about the future, even if precise calculations about what lies ahead result from this process, triggers anxiety and dread.

Uncertainty, Probability, Hope, and Fear

In his discussion of direct passions in book 2 of the *Treatise*, Hume openly confronts the psychological effects of uncertainty and probability, and the conclusion he draws is a familiar one to readers of seventeenth- and eighteenth-century accounts of epistemology and politics. Uncertainty is unnerving at best, painful at worst.[15] In particular, Hume's attention to the countervailing passions of fear and hope produces a thoughtful rendering of how human beings register uncertainty emotionally. As he explains, hope and fear are essentially products of uncertainty: " 'Tis evident, that the very same event, which by its certainty would produce grief or joy, gives always rise to fear or hope, when only probable and uncertain" (*T*, 2.3.9.9, 281). For Hume, those who contemplate the future are pulled between the poles of these opposing passions. As the calculation of future outcomes is split between desirable possibilities and unwanted ones, so is the emotional state of the person doing the calculating split between the instinctive impulses to hope and to fear. Whether individuals find themselves giving in to one passion more strongly than the other depends, in part, on what probable outcome they see in the future.

Hume spends a good part of this section of the *Treatise* working over this phenomenon, to explain that hope and fear exist together in people when they consider an uncertain future event. Hume postulates that contrary future-oriented passions like hope and fear—and their corollary passions in present time, joy and grief—may have three different kinds of relationships. First, he notices that joy and grief may exist together in the same person as present reactions to events. If they arise from different objects, they may coexist in a person with no effect. Hume suggests that, in the present, if someone is at once joyful regarding a welcome event and sorrowful over a loss, these two feelings sit together like "two opposite liquors in different bottles, which have no influence on each other" (*T*, 2.3.9.17, 283). Second, if someone experiences an event of a mixed character, such that it brings inseparable joy and grief, Hume thinks the two passions destroy each other and leave behind a feeling of indifference.

The third possibility is the one Hume gives the most attention to and the one most relevant to the concerns of this chapter, as it explains how future events stir the passions. When we have not yet experienced an event but know that it could happen, we tack back and forth between considering opposite possible outcomes based on past experiences. While doing this cognitive work, we feel joy, and then grief, and then joy again, and so on. These opposing feelings do not dispel quickly after our minds waver; like the notes produced by plucking the strings of a musical instrument, the feelings persist well past the initial idea that produces them (*T*, 2.3.9.16, 283). Hence joy and grief are never totally resolved for the probabilistic thinker. While a person waits for the unknown event to manifest, these feelings intermingle uneasily to generate something new—a tense mixture of hope and fear. Hume notes that these two passions will not exist in even balance in situations of uncertain outcome. Whether we lean more toward hope or fear will depend on the precision of our calculation—our degrees of certainty regarding whether probable events will bring joy or sorrow. If we begin to anticipate an uncertain future event as a joyous one, we increasingly feel hopeful; if not, we are prone to a heightening sense of fear.

Probable events are thus a common source of hope or fear, but Hume broadens his account of these passions by claiming that people also experience them when an event is certain but they are uncertain about their own judgment of it. To take Hume's example, a man imprisoned and sentenced to the rack knows with certainty that he will soon experience something horrible, and his passionate response should be pure grief, as the event is known and practically guaranteed. But Hume thinks this unalloyed response is unlikely. Rather, "the mind continually rejects [the certain evil] with horror, while it continually presses in upon the thought" (*T*, 2.3.9.24, 284). Though the punishment itself is fixed, barring accident, the prisoner's mind cannot quite settle on it, and what he feels from this fluctuation is tantamount to uncertainty. Hence, he never properly grieves and is left only to sit with the anticipatory passion of fear.

At this point in Hume's analysis in the *Treatise*, we can observe a tonal shift toward a darker, more troubling account of how it feels to live in a world that affords little certainty. In an important modification to his initial claim that people are pulled between hope and fear by uncertainty and might expect to feel either one depending on the particular case at hand, Hume ultimately emphasizes that fear repeatedly crowds out what hope anyone might hold for the future and its coming events. The human capacity to hope for desirable outcomes suddenly drops out of Hume's story, as he begins to theorize a tighter connection between uncertain knowledge and fear. Fear, rather than hope, becomes the more common response to a probable future that remains as yet unknown.

Hume begins down this less sanguine path by noting a disparity between his theory of the relationship between probability and the direct passions and his observations on how living with uncertainty actually feels for most people. Given that both good and bad outcomes are probable in the future, one might think that people would experience future-oriented passions like hope and fear in equal, or relatively equal, measure over the long term. That is, sometimes people are compelled to face the future with hope, and sometimes with fear, depending on what they believe is coming. This probable knowledge can even be relatively precise, which should correspond to one particular passion over the other in the immediate term, and relative balance over the long term as people figure different probabilities for both wanted and unwanted future events. But Hume thinks not; in fact, he concludes that over the course of their lives, on balance people mostly feel fearful about the future.

This observation is something of a mystery for Hume to solve, as he points out that "uncertainty is, indeed, in one respect as nearly ally'd to hope as to fear, since it makes an essential part in the composition of the former passion" (T, 2.3.9.27, 285). This leads him to wonder why uncertainty so rarely yields to hope and instead seems to generate predominantly fear and anxiety across cases, even in instances when probability points clearly to a desirable or pleasant future outcome (T, 2.3.9.28–29, 285–86).[16] The conclusion Hume draws is that uncertainty about the future and individuals' reaction to it is *always* psychologically costly. This is true, he thinks, with uncertain outcomes as well as when people are left to anticipate all-but-certain outcomes, even good outcomes they desire. Fear has a strong pull on people when they face the future, and little can be done to relieve it.

Hume's judgment is thus that anticipating the unknown and the unpredictable results in debilitating fear. This claim rests on a particular view of human beings—while people can face the future with some precision and reliability, they are still ill equipped to cope with surprises, accidents, and the unexpected. As he puts it, "every thing that is unexpected affrights us" (T, 2.3.9.26, 285). Unfortunately, as Hume has established, everyone lives with the unexpected daily. Not only must people think and act in a contingent world that often defies prediction, but even the most reliable claims about the future are tinged with a nagging uncertainty. The problem here does not seem to be one of character, as Hume rejects the idea that human beings are simply timid creatures who cannot face an unknown future with fortitude. Rather, the trouble seems to be cognitive. Hume notes that the unexpected or not yet experienced always delivers a surprise, which triggers mental commotion, making people uneasy.[17] This uneasiness—produced in equal measure by both good and bad present or projected outcomes—is so turbulent that it resembles fear, and eventually "this image of fear naturally converts into the thing itself," making the observer *actually* afraid (T, 2.3.9.26, 285). Even when people have good reason to be hopeful about the future, they are overcome by the fear or anxiety produced by the simple fact of their own uncertainty. When living with uncertainty, as everyone must, individuals have trouble *feeling* the difference between facing the future armed with rather precise expectations of what is probable and groping blindly in a world of pure uncertainty.

Hume's discussion of fear emphasizes that living in an unpredictable world is hard and frequently unpleasant. As he notes, "In the common affairs of life, where we feel and are penetrated with the solidity of the subject, nothing can be more disagreeable than fear and terror; and 'tis only in dramatic performances and religious discourses, that they ever give pleasure" (T, 1.3.9.15, 79). In spite of the work Hume has done to show that people may register either hope or fear when pondering the future, his final point is that most people are left to cope with fear and anxiety.[18] The implication of Hume's analysis, in the end, seems to be that the very act of contemplating the future makes people fearful. This bears directly on the question of the human orientation to risk, and, I argue, Hume uses the assumption that risk and fear go hand in hand to guide his analysis of commerce.[19]

In the rest of this chapter, I argue that Hume's depiction of probability and fear shapes his treatment of commercial subjectivity and risk taking. He figures the active, commercial subject as one immersed in the activity of probabilistic calculation for the future and thus mired in the dread of uncertainty. If Hume's project is to "show [readers] how [they] are to get on with [their] lives" and conduct their affairs under persistent uncertainty of varying degrees, he must find a way to persuade them to act without buckling under the weight of fear.[20] For Hume, this "getting on" is tightly linked to the practice of commerce, as exchange of all kinds is the core activity that constitutes projects of human flourishing. But commerce also involves risk at the hands of trading partners, the elements, and a complex system of manufacture and exchange in which not everything can be known conclusively in advance.

To promote action against the backdrop of uncertainty to his readers, Hume must switch genres. His essays, quite distinct in style and tone from his more abstract philosophical writings, offer a way forward, particularly for those actors he is most concerned with—participants in commercial society. For commercial actors to proceed with their risky ventures, they require some assurance that their endeavors can result in gain rather than loss. Hume seeks to encourage risk taking as integral to exploiting the possibilities of trade, assuming that the uncertain character of commerce is painful for his readers and might stop them from moving forward productively. He works to assuage fears that the system of trade is so unpredictable as to be not worth the risk. He does so by offering the most certain form of knowledge he can—a proof about the long-term steadiness of global trade, which he hopes will calm fears about its volatility and risk. Interestingly, he embeds this proof in a form of writing that he thinks cultivates a relationship of trust between philosopher and readers.

Hume's Essays: Instantiating a Balance of Intellectual Trade

Hume's turn to the essay form provides an antidote to the fear he diagnoses as a symptom of a commercial society animated by risky and future-oriented economic practices. His *Treatise*, analyzed so carefully by many for its rich account of probability and the passions, had a disappointing initial public reception, as Hume noted in "My Own Life," when he famously admitted that it "fell dead-born from the press" (*T*, xviii)."[21] Hume's evaluations of different species of philosophy in *An Enquiry Concerning Human Understanding* admit a corresponding worry about the lack of durability of "abstruse," or abstract, philosophy in public life: however correct philosophy's precepts might be, it is dismissed all too easily, he thinks. The essayist, however, is appreciated more fully than the philosopher for his efforts to entertain common sense and to converse with a reading public. Hence Hume's observation that in the future, "Addison, perhaps, will be read with pleasure, while Locke shall be entirely forgotten" (*EHU*, 1.4, 5). Leaving aside the question of whether Hume was right about the staying power of the essay over the treatise, his turn to the essay form need not be interpreted as a ploy to stay in the public eye after the failure of his first book, a member of the aforementioned species of "abstruse" philosophical works. Rather, we should read his essays as part of a sincere effort to produce knowledge that might help along a reading public bent on the business of living, a public that can do no better than to use probable belief as a guide to acting in the present with an eye to the future.[22] For a commercial society saturated in risk, the essay can provide welcome psychological assistance for actors who are neither of wholly abstract mind nor purely passionate disposition. Hume tries to lend this kind of assistance in his essays, particularly his essays on commerce, by preparing his readers to live well against a backdrop of uncertainty and to take better risks.

The model philosopher turns out to be a figure who strikes a balance between being what Hume calls a "mere philosopher," who "lives remote from communication with mankind and is wrapped up in principles and notions equally remote from their comprehension," and being a "mere ignorant," who resists any exposure to advancements in the sciences as they develop and sticks to his own passionate judgments of particular events. Hume argues that "the most perfect character is supposed to lie between those extremes; retaining an equal ability and taste for books, company, and business; preserving in conversation that discernment and delicacy which arise from polite letters; and in business, that probity and accuracy which are the natural results of a just philosophy" (*EHU*, 1.5, 5).[23] This "just" philosophy is grounded primarily in human sociability and action. It cultivates the abilities of readers to reflect more critically on their own experiences by reading about those of others, and in turn to draw on their own experiences and store of knowledge to judge the contribution of the philosopher. The essay genre cultivates practice of intellectual exchange and credit, and it builds a trusting relationship between reader and writer, such that new ideas can be tested and worked through.[24]

Hume's essays, and also his famed *History of England*, perform this work of a more "just philosophy" in two related ways. First, they add to the general stock of experiential knowledge for readers to improve their practice of thinking probabilistically. Second, they show readers in a more conversational way what Hume established in the *Treatise*—that their particular or singular experiences are rarely enough to support claims to reliable or precise probabilistic knowledge.[25] The essayist does this work by serving as a broker, or kind of middleman, sent from the world of philosophy to mediate and trade in the social world. In a fine metaphor drawing on images of diplomacy and commerce, Hume explains what he takes to be his role as an essayist:

> I cannot but consider myself as a Kind of Resident or Ambassador from the Dominions of Learning to those of Conversation; and shall think it my constant Duty to promote a good Correspondence betwixt these two States, which *have so great a Dependence on each other*. I shall give Intelligence to the Learned of whatever passes in Company, and shall endeavour to import into Company whatever Commodities I find in my native Country proper for their Use and Entertainment. The Balance of Trade we need not be jealous of, nor will there be any Difficulty to preserve it on both Sides. The Materials of this Commerce must chiefly be furnish'd by Conversation and common Life; the Manufacturing of them alone belongs to Learning. (*EMPL*, 535; emphasis added)

Here knowledge production is figured as commerce, which would have been known to Hume's contemporaries as a flow of goods *and* communication. The essayist Hume is an expatriate or diplomat from the world of experimental philosophical practice who opens routes of exchange between the already interdependent social world and philosophy. Common life provides the raw material—experience—that can only be elicited through conversation. Hume transports these materials back "home" for conversion into the kinds of arguments that result from what he elsewhere calls a "durable and useful" skeptical experimental philosophy (*EHU,* 12. 24, 140). Significantly, he frames this exchange as a risk-free, positive-sum one that issues in profit on both sides, in a metaphor that prefigures the kind of argument he will make about the positive-sum experience of free trade in his essays on commerce.[26] Even in describing the practice of just philosophy, Hume has something critical to say about how readers should orient themselves toward binding together with strangers in the face of risk and uncertainty, and urges them to see exchange as ultimately quite productive for all parties involved.

That said, the character and form of the knowledge that Hume imports into his "company" of readers is variable, at least as he writes about it in the essays. Pertaining to one of the riskiest terrains for his readers, political life, Hume offers a study in contrasts. In two of his essays on politics, "That Politics May Be Reduced to a Science" and "Of Civil Liberty," we find an exploration of whether it is possible to arrive at general principles about political life that are certain. In the former essay, Hume suggests that the knowledge of politics at this point amounts to proof rather than probability. He claims that "politics admits of general truths, which are invariable by the humour or education either of subject or sovereign." Elsewhere he also makes mention of "eternal political truths that no time nor accidents can vary" (*EMPL,* 18). Thus political knowledge is as secure as experiential knowledge can be. Readers should be as startled to discover that the general rules, or precepts, governing politics are false as they would be to wake up at noon to find that the sun never rose. This type of knowledge—a proof—is possible with respect to politics in part because institutions and laws are so robust; they have "so little dependence . . . on the humours and tempers of men, that consequences almost as general and certain may *sometimes* be deduced from them, as any which the mathematical sciences afford us" (*EMPL,* 16).[27] While Hume is arguing that political knowledge can be known with almost perfect certainty, the qualifier "sometimes" is important here.

In "Of Civil Liberty," Hume's claim that the principles of politics have the status of proof is tempered. Here he is more pessimistic about the possibility of offering a useful and satisfying science of politics rooted in proof—at least for the time being. He explains:

I am apt . . . to entertain a suspicion that the world is still too young to fix many general truths in politics, which will remain true to the latest posterity. We have not as yet had experience of three thousand years; so that not only that art of reasoning is still imperfect in this science, as in all others, but we even want sufficient materials upon which we can reason. (*EMPL*, 87).

A study of politics runs up against the same difficulty that Hume finds in all sciences—the limits of knowledge rooted in experience. But beyond this, his claim is that politics offers insufficient materials, and the source of this insufficiency is time.[28] There has not yet been enough time to gather the requisite experiential materials that might allow the political scientist to generate the kinds of proofs that Hume thinks people can "sometimes" use to make practically certain claims about politics (of the kind he offers in "That Politics May Be Reduced to a Science"). Read together, these two essays imply that the pursuit of political knowledge might very well generate a useful set of proofs because of the stability of institutions and laws, but it is still too soon to tell. To compound this problem, it is impossible to know with certainty *when* the time will come that precepts are more proof than mere probability.

Hume published these two essays, with their disparate accounts of whether the study of politics has issued (or ever will issue) general laws or proof and their seemingly clashing takes on the question of political knowledge, together in several editions of his essay collections. This deliberate contrast reflects something essential about Hume's own philosophical practice as an essayist. It establishes him as a trustworthy practitioner of his own philosophical commitments as an experimentalist, and it creates an opening for collaboration with readers. Hume invites his readerly audience into the process of producing stable political knowledge, encouraging them to ponder the shifts of political life and perhaps contribute to the store of information that the philosopher might use to produce usable precepts concerning politics over time.[29] These two political essays thus initiate a process of learning and balance, albeit one that is unlikely to result in any certain proof any time soon.

This balancing and exchanging of differing perspectives and experiences is part of Hume's practice of mitigated skepticism, a challenging approach to knowledge production, for all the reasons his early reflections on probability suggest. In the *Enquiry Concerning Human Understanding*, he notes that this practice of intellectual exchange and open-minded balance is hard to countenance for most people:

The greater part of mankind are naturally apt to be affirmative and dogmatical in their opinions; and while they see objects only on one side, and have no idea of any counterpoising argument, they throw themselves precipitately into the principles, to which they are inclined; nor have they any indulgence for those who entertain opposite sentiments. To hesitate or *balance* perplexes their understanding, checks their passion, and suspends their action. They are, therefore, impatient till they escape from a state, which to them is so uneasy: and they think, that they could never remove themselves far enough from it, by the violence of their affirmations and obstinacy of their belief. But could such dogmatical reasoners become sensible of the strange infirmities of human understanding, even in its most perfect state, and when most accurate and cautious in its determinations; such a reflection would naturally inspire them with more modesty and reserve, and diminish their fond opinion of themselves, and their prejudice against antagonists. (*EHU*, 12.24, 141; emphasis added)

Hume's sensitivity to the uneasiness created by uncertainty manifests here as an explanation for why people fall into the trap of "dogmatical" reasoning, which prevents intellectual exchange of experience and conversation, and stymies the kinds of modest, probable claims such exchanges can produce. The struggle to "balance" is often jettisoned altogether as too difficult, but it is, as I argue in this chapter, an important orientation for Hume's commercial public to adopt.

The interplay of Hume's two essays on politics supports an interpretation of his turn to the essay form as a way of inaugurating a process of exchange between the "learned" and the "conversable" worlds, in which questions are open and experience is pooled and appraised for the purpose of generating reliable philosophical probabilities. In "Of Civil Liberty," Hume suggests that the changing political world requires collecting more observations to advance and sharpen probabilistic reasoning about the political future. He also provides an example of one urgent project that is especially relevant for this chapter's consideration of the risks of trade. He notices that trade did not become a concern of states until the seventeenth century, and thus even the most able historian cannot yet assemble enough experiential material to formulate general precepts about trade that might withstand accident or contingency (*EMPL*, 99). Thus many commercial actors face the risky ventures that are part of trade armed only with mere probabilities, and the process of calculating these probabilities or risks induces dread, as Hume has already explained. With this in mind, he offers an intervention, which we can see in his more explicitly economic essays.

Hume takes three key steps forward on the project of distilling general principles about trade in economic essays on commerce, especially in "Of the Balance of Trade." First, he suggests that his economic essays, although rich in historical detail, can also highlight some general precepts about political economy that will correct or temper the particular beliefs of his readers. Hume here claims to be importing the philosopher's "commodity" for men of commerce, and perhaps also for politicians managing a commercial state, to consume—general proofs about the course of commerce, particularly international trade. Second, he offers a critique of mercantilism, largely for its parochial and risk-averse orientation toward the practice of trade. His critique harkens back to the two qualifiers he attaches to his account of probability in the *Treatise*: that uncertainty creates cognitive turbulence, which converts easily into fear and then risk-averse behavior; and that unphilosophical probabilities have a way of eroding proof into mere probability. The claim here is that perhaps commercial actors' judgment is clouded by passion and prejudice when it comes to figuring risk. Third, he floats a proof that might correct the prejudices of many readers regarding the risks of trade: an argument that international trade can be self-stabilizing. This last point is extremely important, for it arms a trepidatious commercial society with the knowledge it needs to brook risk now and maintain some hope for the future. Informed by his own work on probability and fear, Hume assumes that commercial subjectivity is marked by aversion to risk, largely because the commercial actor cannot quite *feel* the difference between probable outcomes in his commercial endeavors and sheer uncertainty. Hume's project is to turn the commercial actor back to taking well-chosen risks.

A Balancing Trade: Hume on Commerce and the Assumption of Risk

At the start of his essay "Of Commerce," Hume insists that he has general knowledge of political economy to offer his readers, presumably practitioners of trade and manufacture themselves. To begin, he draws a distinction between his labor and theirs, in terms of the kinds of reasoning they respectively pursue. As he explains:

> When a man deliberates concerning his conduct in any *particular* affair, and forms schemes in politics, trade, oeconomy, or any business in life, he never ought to draw his arguments too fine, or connect too long a chain of consequences together. Something is sure to happen, that will disconcert his reasoning, and produce an event different from what he expected. (*EMPL*, 254)

Here Hume views the affairs and reasoning of the man of action with a sympathetic eye, noting that it is perhaps imprudent for him to plan too far ahead, as some unexpected contingency is sure to undo his expectations and rattle him. Hume later reflects that political and commercial actors have much in common with the "bulk of mankind" on this count. Most people are not well positioned to look past their own immediate conditions to formulate universal and nearly certain principles that move too far beyond their particular circumstances.

Fortunately, Hume's reasoning, like that of other philosophers, is oriented toward the general, and so he has something to offer his readers. In his economic essays, he works to establish general principles about commerce, principles that "if just and sound, must always prevail in the general course of things, though they *may fail in particular cases*" (*EMPL*, 254; emphasis added). This is Hume's trade, and he expects that some of the principles he puts up for exchange will be uncommon and hence unsettling. Thus he begins his collection of work on commerce with a plea to his readers to give his offerings a fair chance, with the caveats that they will be unusual and may not hold in every particular case. That they can hold over the long term, though, is what makes them valuable to Hume's readers, who must engage the vicissitudes of the practical world of commerce—with all its flux, risk, and uncertainty—on a daily basis. Hume asks readers to use his arguments to sustain themselves in this practice. He suggests that while the probabilities they calculate regarding commercial practices might appear correct in the short term, there is a more general view of commerce to keep in mind, one that might expose these judgments as shortsighted motivations for what turn out to be imprudent actions.

Hume analyzes mercantilism as a varied system of economic thought and practice that is characterized by a short-term outlook, and he frames it as an approach to political economy that—mired in fear of uncertainty—takes a worrisome approach to risk.[30] The mercantilist perspective, he suggests, seeks always either to displace risk or to offset or eliminate the downsides of risk. This perspective, he thinks, moves traders to confine their exchanges to local and, if possible, face-to-face interactions in town. Understandably, everyone wants to deal with known partners as much as possible, in the interest of having more certainty about possible outcomes. In international trade, a field in which this direct approach is frequently impossible, traders seek to reduce the uncertainty of commerce by banding into large trading companies, and then by either working with or pressuring the state to suppress competition and direct the flow of trade to their advantage.[31] Hume documents one instance of this phenomenon in the fifth volume of his *History of England*, where he considers Elizabeth I's attempt to open the wool trade and notes how this effort was met with resistance:

> The company of merchant-adventurers, by their patents, possessed the sole commerce of woolen-goods, though the staple of the kingdom. An attempt made during the reign of Elizabeth to lay open this important trade had been attended with bad consequences for a time, by a conspiracy of the merchant-adventurers, not to make any purchases of the cloth: and the queen immediately restored them their cloth.
>
> It was the groundless fear of a like accident that enslaved the nation to those exclusive companies, which confined so much every branch of commerce and industry. (*HE*, 5, 143–44)

Trading companies were unwilling to open the channels of the cloth trade and introduce greater uncertainty and more risk into their commercial practices. This brief example illuminates a pervasive attitude toward trade as a zero-sum endeavor and hence a high-risk venture, with clear winners and losers emerging from a wide pool of commercial actors with limited information and probable knowledge. As with all uncertain and risky enterprises, more open trade could excite hope or fear, depending on the calculation of the probability of gain or loss. After all, by this calculus, *some* winner will emerge. But it is notable that Hume registers only the fear and anxiety of merchants in his retelling of the conflict; the prospect of open trade seems too risky, and the probability calculation of failure *or* success itself generates worry and a corresponding effort to control the flow of trade.

Hume diagnoses this orientation to the prospect of open commerce as pathological, a problem he explores in more general terms in his two essays "Of the Balance of Trade" and "Of the Jealousy of Trade." In both essays, Hume seeks to correct a parochial approach to trade with a more general theory of trade. In effect, he tries to calm two particular fears in wide circulation: first, that if a trading state imports more than it exports, the national supply of hard currency will deteriorate; and second, that free trade among states will advance production abroad at the expense of industry at home. These fears animated the policies of both sophisticated and unsophisticated trading states, creating a trading climate of anxiety and competition that produced pathological ends, by Hume's lights. As Hume says early in "Of the Balance of Trade," those who seek to maintain a positive balance of trade by curbing exports do not realize that "in this prohibition, they act directly contrary to their intention; and that the more is exported of any commodity, the more will be raised at home, of which they themselves will always have the first offer" (*EMPL*, 308). This "strong jealousy with regard to a balance of trade, and a fear, that all their gold and silver may be leaving them," dominated trade policy even in states that understood the flow of commerce and the principles of supply and demand quite well (*EMPL*, 309).

Why, then, this "groundless fear" of the downsides of open trade? Hume suggests that the fear stems in part from the unreliability of information available to merchants who have to reason probabilistically about likely trade outcomes. Customhouse records tracking the outflow of goods; the fluctuating rates of exchange; and records of production, commerce, and exports from other nations were shaky sources, according to Hume. He suggests that nearly anyone can generate whatever projection about commerce he wants based on the "uncertain facts and suppositions" at hand when it comes to trade. Presumably, then, even the most precise calculations of probable success or failure in international trade will produce uncertain or even quite malleable results, because the key sources of information are themselves unreliable. According to Hume's account of the relationship between uncertainty and fear, such a process is doubly likely to result in fear of the worst possible outcome and ultimately issue in behavior that shuns risk (*EMPL*, 310–11). Curiously, Hume's solution to this problem is not to promote a more careful, detailed, and secure system of recording the to and fro of commerce—a system that might generate more security for traders risking their fortunes in the practice of international trade. Instead, he proposes a more general solution—adopting a different perspective on the commercial system itself.[32]

Hume argues that political economy needs to be liberated from the particularistic impulses that shape it, especially the urge to avoid loss in trade. In his essays on political economy, he urges his readers to step back from their particular concerns and take a more general view of trade as a positive-sum game in which *both* partners might win in the long term. Recall that this echoes his description of the kind of intellectual exchange he sets up with his readers, too—a trading partnership in which no one loses and everyone benefits. As part of this effort, he imports the following idea to his readers, men of business: the economy very well might self-stabilize if freed of the policies employed by a risk-averse merchant class bent on maintaining a positive balance of trade.

Against some mercantilist policies that work to diminish the downsides of risky commercial endeavors, Hume is instead advocating the embrace of a free trade system that, though no more risky itself, encourages a more open *attitude* to risk taking. Hume never claims that there is *no* probability of loss in the open system he advocates; what he does suggest is that the risk of loss needs to be interpreted in the wider context of international free trade—a context in which, in the long term, an open system produces overall gains for all comers, on balance.[33] Hume thus tries to reorient his readers to a new psychology of risk taking that emphasizes the idea of no *long*-term loss in an open system of international trade. As he notes, the emphatic belief that one is on the wrong end of a trade balance can "never be refuted by a particular detail of all the exports, which counterbalance the imports." Perhaps this is why Hume does not aim to solve the problem at the level of detail. Instead of calling for a wholesale reconstruction of how information is managed in the commercial world, he makes a general argument that there simply *is* no wrong end of the balance, no long-term loss of a country's money or resulting power, "as long as [it] preserve[s] [its] people and [its] industry" and participates in open trade (*EMPL*, 311).[34] Note that Hume moves back from concern for the individual commercial actor as a risk taker here, for the aim of his economic writings is "to clarify the principles behind a *state's* rising powers and the prospering of a *nation*."[35] So, he demands that his readers think more broadly in two ways: they must take a longer view of time and a wider view of their social and political context as economic actors.

Hume's general argument runs like this: In any given country, prices of goods depend on the ratio of commodities produced to the amount of money in circulation. As he puts it in "Of Money," "Encrease the commodities, they become cheaper; encrease the money, they rise in their value. As, on the other hand, a diminution of the former, and that of the latter, have contrary tendencies" (*EMPL*, 290). In exchange between two countries—as long as people and industry are prioritized, as Hume suggests they must be—a shift in the quantity of money in the economy would generate a price movement. This movement in price would eventually destroy or cancel out the results of the disturbance in available money if the country continued its import/export trade.

Hume also offers a hypothetical in support of the model. If the hard currency of Britain were to multiply dramatically overnight, labor and commodities would become so expensive that none of her neighbors would be able to buy from her. In the meantime, their goods would become so relatively inexpensive that importing them would be irresistible, and hence the surplus money would flow out of Britain until the balance between her and her trading partners was restored (*EMPL*, 311).[36] Hume repeatedly emphasizes that a balance will always be restored in the system, so as to alleviate the fears and prejudices that drive the current zero-sum approaches to risk taking. His emphasis works to alleviate the two fears most widely in circulation—the fear of depletion in national supplies of hard currency and the fear of decline in the production of goods at home. By Hume's analysis, opening trade should, at the very least, maintain the status quo and perhaps bring even more desirable results on both fronts.

Hume thus attempts to theorize a self-regulating system in which "money [is preserved] nearly proportionable to the art and industry of each nation" over the long term, an account that provides an alternate interpretation of political economy to the one he criticizes. To neutralize the particular episodes that might tempt men of trade to reject his general theory on the basis of temporary loss, he draws an analogy between the flow of money and a phenomenon theorized in the natural sciences:

> All water, wherever it communicates, remains *always at a level*. Ask naturalists the reason: they tell you, that, were it to be raised in any one place, the superior gravity of that part not being balanced, must depress it, till it meet a counterpoise; and that the same cause, which redresses the inequality when it happens, must for ever prevent it, *without some violent external operation*. (*EMPL*, 312; emphasis added)

This is an intriguing and authoritative move. Here Hume compares the mechanism that balances the flow of money to gravity, which he elsewhere describes as a certainty in the natural world. As the level of water is always smoothed over in time, so too will the flow of currency and the system of trade be smoothed into exchanges of mutual gain and benefit, as long as readers resist the urge to impose "some violent external operation," perhaps as a result of "groundless fear" of probable loss in the short term. By drawing on an authoritative proof from the natural sciences, Hume argues by analogy for a self-regulating system that will benefit all parties if they resist the urge to control it through external means.[37]

Hume's purpose in the essays, I argue, is to make his readers less risk averse when it comes to commerce, especially trade. The essays on trade and commerce suggest that the unwillingness of commercial actors to shoulder the burdens of risky economic ventures can result in material loss in the long term. Or, at the very least, Hume speculates that risk aversion produces policies and practices that cut off the possibility of mutual long-term material *gain* for all parties involved. For these reasons, he urges his readers to take prudent chances in their economic lives, even bearing short-term difficulties with an eye to the future, presumably by eschewing the fearful attitudes and doctrines in circulation. But the hope of material gain is not the only motivation for a less fearful, less conservative approach to commercial practices and partnerships. For Hume, an open approach to commerce is tightly connected to flourishing in many spheres, as he reminds his readers in "Of the Refinement of the Arts," where he argues that improvements in economic practice yield all kinds of political, social, and intellectual goods for members of a commercial society. Hence, how human beings manage their aversion to risk is a critical question for Hume, one picked up by his friend Adam Smith, who confronts the same problem in *The Wealth of Nations*, his critique of the existing political economy.

Conclusion

Even though Hume rarely uses the word "risk" in his writings, I have argued in this chapter that he is a sophisticated early theorist of risk. One element of Hume's work that is especially valuable for the study of risk is his careful parsing of probability, followed by his insight that the practice of probabilistic reasoning does not make commercial actors confident in the risks they might take, but instead reminds them of the persistence of uncertainty and stirs them to fear. Hume effectively establishes the risk-taking subject as a fearful one, oriented to loss. As such, his work suggests that efforts to confront and manage risk must also entail efforts to govern and shape commercial actors into more hopeful sorts, who will either take on more risks or be willing to shoulder the short-term losses that might well accompany risky commercial endeavors.

Hume takes a step toward the cultivation of hope by creating a climate of trust and credit in something of an epistemological vacuum. Part of the reason commercial actors are so reluctant to take risks or deal with the downsides of commercial risk taking is a real dearth of reliable information about far-flung trading partners or past commercial practices and outcomes. Sympathetic to these difficulties, Hume invites his readers to trust him and take a step back to look at the entire system. He argues for a self-regulating, trustworthy system and relies on his own credit as a public intellectual to make this case. He also reorients commercial actors to the project of focusing on the wealth of the nation-state, not on the wealth of the individual or the trading company. Thus his work explores how governing the risks of international trade amounts to reshaping risk-taking subjects into the sort of people who will take more calculated risks and perhaps even bear up under the weight of more losses, by orienting them toward hope for a better future in the longer term and for a broader public. In the next chapter, I explore how Hume's friend Adam Smith continued to think about the problem Hume suggests—that risk-taking subjects are not as properly attuned to sacrifice as they could be, nor in possession of the right sort of character to bear with the challenges of a commercial society saturated in risk.

CHAPTER FIVE

ADVENTUROUS SPIRITS AND CLAMORING SOPHISTS

Smith on the Problem of Risk in Political Economy

Adam Smith's body of work on commercial society provides a sustained engagement with the problem of how to confront risk. Although he may appear to engage with the problem of risk only episodically, I argue that reading his reflections together reveals that he held an appropriately multidimensional conception of risk, and one that is true to its complexity as a problem. Smith often hews very closely to how we define risk now, as a matter of probabilistic or predictive knowledge about an unknown future, produced by cognitive habits of experiential reasoning and calculation, perhaps following the insights of his friend Hume. But, much as we often do now, he sometimes uses the word "risk" when his analysis might be better served by terms like "danger" or "harm"; at other points still, he gives risk a positive valence, linking it to the pursuit of adventure, pleasure, and profit. Smith's work thus reflects the ubiquity of risk in the late eighteenth century and demonstrates that it was by then a multifaceted concept, open to interpretation and contest.

Beyond offering a complex account of the meaning of risk, Smith also analyzes different approaches to managing the problem of risk, which add up to a depiction of commercial nation-states as effectively saturated with risk. One particularly compelling feature of Smith's work is that he examines the pervasiveness of risk in a wide variety of commercial contexts—individual character and behavior, group mentalities and behaviors, institutions, and public policies. First, he thinks carefully about the individual's confrontations with risk, particularly in the sphere of political economy. What orientation ought the individual have to economic risk? Is risk an opportunity to be seized in the interest of profit and adventure, or a dangerous threat to security and prosperity? Smith thinks especially critically about the risks different kinds of individuals take in the context of late eighteenth-century commercial society, and evaluates the results as decidedly mixed. Second, Smith considers how membership in a group might shape the individual's orientation to risk, usually with the effect of driving people to take bigger chances under the influence and within the comfort of a group of risk takers. Third, Smith contemplates whether the design of particular institutions can alter the individual's orientation to risk. In particular, he analyzes how the structures of corporations—trading companies especially—can mitigate or obscure the risks borne by their members, thus supporting more reckless decision-making practices in the short term, with often damaging results in the longer term. Finally, he contemplates whether particular policies can enjoin commercial actors to take healthy or "safe" risks (e.g., fixing interest rates), as well as whether particular policies shield some actors from risk at the expense of others (e.g., traders and politicians vis-à-vis laborers and consumers).

Through his very specific considerations of eighteenth-century commercial behavior, institutions, and politics, Smith effectively establishes risk as a permanent feature of late eighteenth-century commerce and politics.[1] His work also captures the ambivalence that characterizes the human encounter with risk. On the one hand, Smith expresses some admiration for bold adventurers who take both reasonable and even outsized risks, such as the commercial trader or the glory-seeking politician. On the other hand, he offers a strong moral criticism of individuals who take these kinds of commercial or political risks, at points holding them alongside "prodigals," who waste resources, and "projectors," who speculate without good odds. We could conclude that Smith is simply inconsistent in his views on risk, or we could attempt to impose a strict moral schematic onto his evaluations of risk-seeking and risk-taking behaviors. I argue, however, that a more nuanced reading of his work suggests that he is simply ambivalent about risk because of its dual capacity for profit and loss, an ambivalence that characterizes both modern and contemporary attempts to live with risk. In his late writings, however, Smith does prescribe one rather old-fashioned virtue to modern commercial actors who must negotiate the inherently conflictual nature of risk—prudence, a supple character trait born of experience and reflection. The choice of prudence, I argue, underscores Smith's intuition that while risk is not a problem that can be solved definitively with precision in the context of commercial society, it must be persistently managed with vigilance. After some engagement with larger-scale efforts to manage risk—institutions and policies—Smith ultimately returns to the microfoundations of risk management, proposing a modest but powerful intervention at the level of individual character.

Risk and the Commercial Subject

Much of Smith's analysis of risk, particularly in *The Wealth of Nations*, engages with the behavior and psychology of the risk-taking individual in commercial society. His point of entry to the individual's engagement with risk is the figure of the merchant or trader and his temperament and behavior. Smith's description of traders in *The Wealth of Nations* can be read as an adventure story—an account of men who dare to confront risk in the interest of bettering their fortunes.[2] He offers a character sketch of them, which reads as a depiction of an economic actor for whom the riskiest of ventures are exciting, pleasurable, and potentially quite profitable. In so doing, Smith emphasizes a notion of risk that is steeped in ideas of adventure, agency, and promise. In a passage meant to emphasize the unusually bold but perhaps shortsighted disposition of the international trader, Smith compares him to another important figure in the political economy, the landlord. He observes that

> upon equal, or nearly equal profits, most men will choose to employ their capitals rather in the improvement and cultivation of land, than either in manufactures or in foreign trade. The man who employs his capital in land, has it more under his view and command, and his fortune is much less liable to accidents than that of the trader, who is obliged frequently to commit it, not only to the winds and the waves, but to the more uncertain elements of human folly and injustice, by giving great credits in distant countries to men, with whose character and situation he can seldom be thoroughly acquainted. The capital of the landlord, on the contrary, which is fixed in the improvement of his land, seems to be as well secured as the nature of human affairs can admit of. (*WN* 3.1.3, 377–78)[3]

Relative to other economic actors in a commercial society, merchants constantly risk their resources to conditions that are more or less uncertain. Overseas trade in particular exposes merchants' fortunes to natural and manmade accidents beyond human control, as well as to the uncertain whims of weather and maritime conditions. To be fair, landowners are also subject to the changing and sometimes unpredictable conditions of nature. But merchants go further, as they also entrust their economic fates to credit relations with relatively unfamiliar business partners, instead of sinking their capital into land development or even large-scale manufacturing, which they could keep under closer surveillance. That merchants should choose this doubly uncertain path "upon equal, or nearly equal profits," reveals a rare but, to Smith, intriguing temperament that seeks out risk, even when more secure courses of action are available.

For this risk-loving actor, Smith also points out that the resulting pay-off of confronting risk boldly may, in the end, be less than imagined. In a discussion of sea trade in book 1 of *The Wealth of Nations*, he observes that while "the ordinary rate of profit rises *more or less* with the risk, [i]t does not, however, seem to rise *in proportion to it*, or so as to compensate it *compleately*" (*WN*, 1.10b.33, 128; emphasis added). The reason for this lies with the risk taker's faulty reasoning—Smith argues that what ultimately undercuts the profit-generating promise of especially precarious economic ventures is an inherent bias in the perception of risk, an inability to interpret probabilities and calculate future outcomes reliably. Every trader, he argues, thinks he will be the exception who proves the rule—the one who overcomes unfavorable conditions and beats poor odds to turn a profit. In this regard, I think we see a real difference between how Hume thinks commercial actors approach risk and what Smith thinks about traders in particular. Smith finds that a "presumptuous hope of success" lures enough people into hazardous economic ventures that the resulting competition drives down profits well below what might compensate for the potential losses involved (*WN*, 1.10b.33, 128). Bold endeavors may thus not bear out their promise in the end, but this is partly because of the attractiveness of risk and its ability to warp traders' efforts to figure the odds.

Smith thus depicts merchants as somewhat rash, and perhaps deeply unrealistic, profiteers in search of immediate gratification, cut from a different cloth than more staid economic actors like small retailers or minor property owners, who patiently improve their holdings incrementally. Merchants are drawn to the riskiest of economic ventures, and this attraction appears to dull rather than refine their capacity to engage in thoughtful calculation of probable outcomes. Despite his scrutiny of them, however, Smith implies that traders may not actually be exceptional on this front, just a more undisciplined sort than most. For most people, the temptation to overvalue their personal ability to risk and win against unfavorable odds is strong, on Smith's reading:

> The over-weening conceit which the greater part of men have of their own abilities, is an antient evil remarked by the philosophers and moralists of all ages. Their absurd presumption in their own good fortune, has been less taken notice of. It is, however, if possible, still more universal. There is *no man living* who, when in tolerable health and spirits, has not some share of it. (*WN*, 1.10b.26, 124; emphasis added)

To Smith, then, everyone has a share of the blind optimism in the face of risk that drives human beings to take all kinds of chances and expect the best. He goes on in the same section to comment, "the chance of gain is by every man more or less over-valued, and the chance of loss is by most men under-valued, and by scarce any man, who is in tolerable health and spirits, valued more than it is worth" (*WN*, 1.10b.26, 124–25). This imbalanced perspective is nowhere more evident than in the young, he argues, whose presumptuous hope of gain outweighs cautious fear of loss when they choose their professions. "Contempt of risk," as Smith puts it, is possessed by everyone, but he observes that some are more prone to indulging this impulse than others, chief among them the youthful and the temperamentally adventurous (*WN*, 1.10b.29, 126). Notably, both the young and the adventurous typically plunge headfirst into trade as a preferred source of livelihood, which brings Smith's general analysis of risk back to a point of intersection with his views on the trader as a special kind of economic actor when it comes to risky behavior.

Smith comments that, once committed to bold economic enterprises, the trader can find ways to offset the risks he must necessarily take. Interestingly, in his endeavors to stay prosperous, he must model his character on the turbulent spirit of his chosen profession and learn to be mercurial. The trader's constantly shifting enterprises are informed, however, by probabilistic reasoning. As Smith explains, the speculative merchant is "a corn merchant this year, and a wine merchant the next, and a sugar, tobacco, or tea merchant the year after. He enters into every trade when he foresees that it is likely to be more than commonly profitable, and he quits it when he foresees that its profits are likely to return to the level of other trades" (*WN*, 1.10b.38, 130). Certainly this account of the ever-changing trades of merchants may be read in the context of Smith's characterization of them as temperamentally unsteady. But their flexibility in choice of trade is not simply a matter of fickle character. Rather, a trader's propensity for shifting quickly to new ventures is sometimes a symptom of skill, knowledge, and prudence—that is, it is strategy. Once merchants choose to make their livelihood by trade, they must be versatile if they are to acquire and secure their fortunes against hazard or loss. Attention to relative stock profits or trends compels a shift in trade if merchants are to turn a profit from year to year. Put another way, they must calculate the potential losses or gains of a particular trade at any given moment and be willing to risk a new venture to protect and build their fortunes. Flexibility, in this case, is not mere unsteadiness but is instead a critical component of prudent and skillful economic practice. And just often enough, this choice to confront risk directly and boldly issues in great returns. Traders who are willing to pursue more speculative and hazardous overseas ventures are often the winners of quick fortunes, in contrast to those slowly amassed over a lifetime by people committed to long-standing and established economic practices.

While traders thus need to be adaptable—to the point of appearing whimsical to an untrained eye—with respect to their particular economic ventures, the best of them also balance the volatile aspects of trade with the cultivation of a stable network of trading partners and creditors. In a longer discussion of how wages correspond to the social trust invested in laborers, Smith notes that traders may again constitute a special category. The usual criteria, like proper education for a specialty (as with medical professionals) or the value of the raw materials entrusted to a worker (as with a jeweler), do not hold for traders, who may not be trained and who use their own stock in trade. Instead, it is the public perception of character that counts for them. Sought-after trading partners will be those who appears successful to their creditors, who judge the traders' "fortune, probity and prudence" by discerning the patterns of their business practices and profits (*WN*, 1.10b.20, 122). Smith notes elsewhere that the practice of trade should, in the successful merchant, inculcate plainly visible habits of "order, oeconomy, and attention" as these can both improve his fortune and shore up his credit with others (*WN*, 3.4.3, 412).[4] As Smith comments in *The Theory of Moral Sentiments*, maintaining a stable fortune in any profession depends on "character and conduct, or upon the confidence, esteem and good-will, which these naturally excite in the people we live with" (*TMS*, 6.1.3, 249). But in *The Wealth of Nations*, Smith argues that social approbation plays an especially critical role for traders. This is particularly true in the case of international trade, which, as Smith points out, is not conducted face to face and may depend more on a good reputation. While merchants necessarily take chances, it also behooves them to be careful and prudent in their dealings, to cultivate their reputations as creditworthy and trustworthy trading partners.

At this point, Smith's reflections on the trader situate him as first among many when it comes to a perception of risk that favors its potential for profit and adventure, a perhaps more extreme manifestation of the risk-loving tendencies that can be found in all people. Traders see their risky professional endeavors predominantly as desirable opportunities to make a quick fortune, with scant attention to looming losses. Smith thus depicts traders largely as a class of economic actors set apart by their skewed orientation to risk, with the caveat that some of them manage the contingencies and risks of trade by governing their affairs systematically and prudently, building a stable network of partners on a foundation of social esteem and mutual trust. These especially prudent traders counter, Smith thinks, the bold confrontation with risk that their profession requires by building systems of provisional but useful knowledge about trade patterns and networks, and by cultivating networks of mutual credit and trust.

Ample evidence suggests, however, that Smith thinks such prudent characters are a rarity in the political economy. In fact, at many points of his analysis, we find representations of the trader as a particularly ungovernable figure, who poses real problems for the stability and flourishing of a commercial society, in terms of both its political economy and its moral economy. Though the earlier parts of *The Wealth of Nations* offer reflections on the trader as a special kind of individual when it comes to the confrontation with risk, when Smith reflects on the political economy as a broader system, he returns to judge the character of traders again, but this time as members of a group. His evaluation of their behavior as a self-conscious *class* of commercial and political actors mostly unfolds in books 4 and 5 of *The Wealth of Nations*, and it is overwhelmingly critical. When traders bind together to confront the risks of their chosen profession, Smith observes, a deep awareness of and aversion to the potential commercial losses invited by trade begins to emerge. This complicates Smith's prior observation that most people have an unwise contempt for risk because they see only the looming profits and exhilarating adventures that come with risky ventures. While traders, when they come together, may not hold a healthy respect for risk taking, they are sharply aware of the threats and losses it can impose, and this perspective shapes their approach to public life in a way that disturbs Smith.

From Risky Ventures to Riskier Venturers

Although Smith finds nothing wrong with protecting one's own economic interests per se and often approves of the wealth and opulence generated by all kinds of commercial activity, he frequently opposes the methods commercial actors employ to achieve wealth and prosperity. He particularly finds fault with the political strategies employed by merchants and traders, engaged in a field of economic risk, to offset loss of capital and keep their own profits as high as possible through artificial means that reverberate throughout the whole system. As his analysis brings to the fore, Smith is relatively tolerant of various individual efforts—including pathological ones—because he expects they will wash out in the end. In *The Wealth of Nations*, Smith notes that "it can seldom happen . . . that the circumstances of a great nation can be much affected either by the prodigality or misconduct of *individuals*; the profusion or imprudence of some being always more than compensated by the frugality and good conduct of others" (*WN*, 2.3.27, 341; emphasis added). Even while Smith criticizes the rather cavalier attitude toward risk that drives some actors in the political economy, he holds out hope that the modest and prudent behavior of others will bring balance to the whole system in the end.

Smith's critical analysis of behavior in a political economy becomes much darker, however, when he sets aside his evaluation of individual actors and turns his attention to groups.[5] He locates real dangers to the prosperity and morality of a commercial society in practices of combination, collusion, and conspiracy. He starts paying attention to these patterns very early in the text, beginning in book 1. Smith warns against trusting "those who live by profit," particularly manufacturers and merchants who collaborate for the purposes of trade (*WN*, 1.11p.10, 266). Mostly, he finds them to be deceptive men of "clamour and sophistry," who deftly persuade other participants in the political economy that their particular interests are in fact the interests of all yet are noticeably "silent with regard to the pernicious effects of their own gains" (*WN*, 1.10c.25, 144; 1.9.24, 115). In fact, Smith concludes book 1 with harsh words for this "order of men . . . who have generally an interest to deceive and even to oppress the publick, and who accordingly have, upon many occasions, both deceived and oppressed it" (*WN*, 1.11p.10, 267).[6] Smith argues that while it is ordinarily in the public interest to widen the market *and* widen competition, "men who live by profit" frequently try to govern the risks of trade by widening the market and narrowing competition.

Nowhere is this more evident than in *The Wealth of Nations*' analysis of the pathologies of mercantile institutions and policies pertaining to international trade. Smith argues that, while individual traders may frequently overvalue their own ability to succeed against the odds while turning a blind eye to the downside of risky economic ventures, groups of traders—particularly those who participate in the ventures of joint-stock companies—are themselves a terrible risk to the political economy. As with Hume's analysis of political economy and trade, Smith's evaluation of mercantile Britain tells a story of deep anxiety about risk and an unwillingness to embrace its threatening side along with its profit potential. In Smith's view, some of the most destructive collective practices and policies of the mercantile system can be traced to this orientation to risk: a willingness to exploit risk for profit, while refusing to take responsibility for any accompanying losses or to make any necessary sacrifices. In particular, Smith notices that as traders are increasingly inclined to take risks in their economic ventures, their pursuit of security grows ever more aggressive. These security-seeking practices move away from the cultivation of private business acumen and toward systematic efforts to control economic policy through political maneuvering and manipulation. Smith begins to figure traders as a self-conscious class of economic subjects, and his analysis of their political and economic practices forms the central critique of *The Wealth of Nations*, a meditation on how risk ought not to be governed in the political economy.

Two of the sharpest and most famous criticisms found in *The Wealth of Nations*—Smith's harsh indictment of joint-stock companies as institutions set up to promote irresponsible risk taking, and his scorn for the "balance of trade" doctrine—suggest that Smith's concern with pathological approaches to risk strongly informs his broad critique of mercantilist approaches to political economy. Smith's critique of joint-stock companies and his effort to dismantle the balance of trade doctrine fall within the purview of his clear disdain for monopolies. But his disapproval of the spirit and practice of monopoly is, at bottom, also a reflection on how living with risk sometimes spurs efforts to control the unknown, with perverse economic, political, and moral consequences. When he analyzes trading companies and the policies they promote, one of his primary concerns is that, in a brazen effort to squeeze all the profits from risky economic ventures without shouldering any prospective losses, traders collude with ambitious and largely ignorant politicians to manipulate the political economy in their favor. The risk of loss does not disappear, however, and Smith is sorry to see it deflected by traders and redistributed among ordinary people, especially consumers. Among the worst offenders, he argues, are joint-stock companies.

Smith's consideration of the pathologies of joint-stock companies—their poor economic practices, their desperate turn to monopoly, and their efforts to procure political power—rests on an insight that they are effectively designed to promote careless risk taking rather than to incentivize cautious or prudent economic decision making. As institutions, they are structured so that a sizable base of stockholders can leave much of the decision making to a board of directors. As a result, Smith notices, most stockholders "seldom pretend to understand any thing of the business of the company; and when the spirit of faction happens not to prevail among them, give themselves no trouble about it, but receive contentedly such half yearly or yearly dividend, as the directors think proper to make to them" (*WN*, 5.1e.18, 741). This amounts to a "total exemption from trouble and from risk, beyond a limited sum" for most of the stockholders, which motivates them to tacitly endorse or simply ignore the risky practices of joint-stock companies, practices they would never try alone or even in a small partnership. In turn, Smith notes that the directors are not especially attentive to business either because they are managing other people's money rather than their own. Free from the "anxious vigilance" with which they might watch their own assets and investments, they tend to take more risks with the goods of their investors (*WN*, 5.1e.18).

Smith thus emphasizes that joint-stock companies are essentially set up for mismanagement, because their structure shields both shareholders and company directors from direct confrontation with the downsides of risk and thus provides them with no sustained opportunity to cultivate the habits of order and economy or the personal networks of credit and trust that might offset risky ventures.[7] While the design of joint-stock companies thus creates something of a moral deficit, by Smith's lights, it also yields undesirable consequences in the political economy. Smith notices that these companies are rarely able to make a profit unless they have managed to secure a monopoly in a particular area of trade. But even (and perhaps especially) when sheltered by monopolistic privilege, they still manage their affairs poorly. As he puts it:

> Negligence and profusion, therefore, must always prevail, more or less, in the management of the affairs of such a company. It is upon

this account that joint stock companies for foreign trade have seldom been able to maintain the competition against private adventurers. They have, accordingly, very seldom succeeded without an exclusive privilege; and frequently have not succeeded with one. Without an exclusive privilege they have commonly mismanaged the trade. With an exclusive privilege they have *both* mismanaged *and* confined it. (*WN*, 5.1e.18, 741)

Smith depicts the men in this relatively small order of company directors as largely reckless and manipulative rather than far sighted and prudent in their efforts to maintain their status as the greatest shareholders in the public good. He faults them twice over—for their poor attention to risk in the internal management of their companies, as well as for their attempts to limit competition and restrict trade to keep themselves afloat amid profound mismanagement, efforts that have far-reaching consequences for others who have not signed on to these enterprises. Among those suffering these consequences are societies of consumers as well as inhabitants of the countries many of these companies end up effectively ruling.[8]

Given that Smith gives some attention to how joint-stock companies acquire "exclusive privilege" in trade, we might situate his critique of them in the stream of his persistent criticism of monopolies more generally. What is significant for the purposes of this chapter, however, is how Smith's analysis of joint-stock companies provides a window into his views on pathological approaches to risk. First, their very design is meant to insulate all participants from the losses that risk may bring—shareholders do not have to confront directly any of the difficult tradeoffs or decisions that come with taking risks in international trade, and directors are one degree removed from loss, given that they are not managing their own money. This attention to the pathologies of joint-stock company management squares with Smith's early accusation that traders are excessively risk loving—in this case, with other people's investments. But his observations about stockholders suggest that many people are afraid to take risks on their own and seek shelter in corporate endeavors, which does *not* square with his claim that almost all people overvalue chances of success. The deeper point of Smith's analysis thus appears to be that all people—even those who are unusually risk averse—might take greater chances and behave less responsibly in groups, particularly when these groups are designed to insulate their members from the sacrifices that risk taking demands. As such, the structure of these joint-stock companies is parasitic on existing human contempt for risk and may cultivate that orientation more broadly.

The problems generated by how joint-stock companies approach risk taking do not remain internal to the companies themselves. Smith also identifies these companies as "prime movers in the system of global commerce," arguing that they have "not only colluded with states, but captured state power" to insulate themselves from both economic competition and political reproach.[9] As such, we might also name them as major culprits in Smith's running commentary on political corruption, which begins in book 1 of *The Wealth of Nations*.[10] This critique of corruption, I argue, is also informed by Smith's insight that risk takers will go to great lengths, and frequently pursue morally or politically suspect measures, to avoid taking responsibility for the downsides of risk.

Smith notes in a critical appraisal of corporation laws and other regulations that even beyond the confines of the structure of joint-stock companies, traders and manufacturers are eager to band together in support of taxes on foreign imports as well as blocks to any price competition that might come from neighboring commercial towns. Their policy interventions raise their profits above what would be "natural" in the context of widened markets and widespread competition and usually go hand in hand with an "absurd" tax on the rest of the public. For these reasons, Smith argues that proposals for structuring trade that come from merchants should be studied carefully, "not only with the most scrupulous, but with the most suspicious attention," by the public and its representatives, who will ultimately bear the costs of the risks these economic actors take when they try to socialize the downsides across a public of consumers (*WN*, 1.11p.10, 267).[11]

Smith does consider a more innocuous explanation for the conflict between profit-seeking traders, along with their political partners, and a public of consumers. He briefly grants traders and manufacturers the benefit of the doubt, noting that their thoughts are so often preoccupied with their particular interests that their judgment of what is best for the whole, even when divulged earnestly (and Smith judges this an inconstant occurrence), is simply unreliable (*WN*, 1.11p.10, 266). Presumably, the sectarian tendencies of these men are also found in other classes of people, all of whom sometimes yield to what skewed perspective tells them. What sets apart merchants and manufacturers, however, is not merely that they have only partial or biased knowledge of the public good because of their overly self-regarding perspective. Rather, Smith claims, they know the public interest all too well and undermine it *intentionally.* He observes that "people of the same trade seldom meet together, even for merriment and diversion, but the conversation ends in a conspiracy against the publick, or in some contrivance to raise prices" (*WN*, 1.10c.27, 145). Smith suggests that this initial instinct to shift the losses that accompany risky business ventures onto consumers eventually hardens into a set of politically pathological attitudes and behavior, such that prodigality supported by plotting becomes the norm in almost all their commercial endeavors, not merely the most risky ones. As such, what begin as merely sectional economic interests eventually become political factions.

Smith's concerns about the transformation of what could be called benign economic interest into political sectarianism, motivated by dread of the downsides of risk, come out strongly in his evaluation of the balance of trade doctrine. In many respects, Smith's account is indebted to the very influential critique supplied by Hume a few decades earlier. Hume's analysis supplies Smith with a core claim regarding what motivates a nation-state's commitment to achieving and maintaining a perpetual positive balance of trade—not reason, but sentiments like fear and jealousy. In Hume's 1742 "Of the Balance of Trade," he notes:

> It is very usual, in nations ignorant of the nature of commerce, to prohibit the exportation of commodities, and to preserve among themselves whatever they think valuable and useful. They do not consider that, in this prohibition, they act directly contrary to their intention; and that the more is exported of any commodity, the more will be raised at home, or which they themselves will always have the first offer. (*EMPL*, 308)

As I argue in the previous chapter, Hume's purpose in "Of the Balance of Trade" is to educate a public anxious about the prospect of free trade and ignorant of its role in a prosperous commercial society. He contends that nations would benefit much more from attending to their people and industries than from focusing on positive trade balances and hoarding hard currency. If trade were opened and its risks confronted with prudence and proper knowledge, the flow of money, goods, and communication should balance itself over time. Hume stresses that it is useless or even potentially harmful to institute an imbalance of this kind artificially, as the balance of trade doctrine endorses (*EMPL*, 311–12). He cautions against giving way to the fear that relatively unrestricted trading with other countries will increase their wealth and industry and render them an existential threat to Britain and her economy. Instead, he persistently claims that domestic industry and prosperity increase by trade with others, and that it is impossible to reap the benefits of trade if surrounded by poor states without improved industry or communication. He tries to persuade his readers that unrestricted commercial relations between states are likely to produce wealth on both sides, and that this relationship is not, and should not be perceived as, zero-sum. In the interest of making his argument, he names jealousy, anxiety, and fear rather than prudence or probabilistic calculation as the motivations for the balance of trade doctrine and suggests that efforts to manipulate and improperly exploit risky open trade may ultimately produce more harm than good. Hume's insights anticipate and inform Smith's own analysis of the balance of trade doctrine, which he reads as motivated by a complicated interaction of reason, sentiment, and vice, produced by a confrontation with risk.

In a famed passage from *The Wealth of Nations*, Smith comments that "nothing . . . can be more absurd than this whole doctrine of the balance of trade, upon which . . . almost all . . . the regulations of commerce are founded" (*WN*, 4.3c.2, 488). In his critique of the doctrine, Smith hews to Hume's arguments very closely, particularly the assertion that it is likely to bear out unfavorable economic consequences for the wealth of a nation and for the well-being of its population of consumers. In the *Lectures on Jurisprudence*, his analysis echoes Hume's:

> The idea of publick opulence consisting in money has been productive of . . . bad effects. Upon this principle most pernicious regulations have been established. These species of commerce which drain us of our money are thought dissadvantageous and these which increase it beneficial; therefore the former are prohibited and the latter encouraged. As France is thought to produce more of the elegancies of life than this country, and as we take much from them and they need little from us, the *balance* of *trade* is against us, and therefore almost all our *trade* with France is prohibited by great taxes and duties on importation. On the other hand, as Spain and Portugal take more of our commodities than we of theirs, the *balance* is in our favours, and this *trade* is not only allowed but encouraged. The absurdity of these regulations will appear on the least reflection. (*LJ*, 511)

The doctrine yields different policy strategies endorsed by trading companies and cabals of merchants, but their efforts usually concentrate on the acquisition of exclusive trading rights with particular partners or on monitoring and restricting the flow of particular imports and exports in and out of their home countries.

To underscore his skepticism about the veracity of the doctrine, Smith gives the example of restricted trade between Britain and France and notes that each country's commitment to maintaining a favorable trade balance against the other has limited its prosperity and nurtured unnecessary hostility. He complains, "And the traders of both countries have announced, *with all the passionate confidence of interested falsehood,* the certain ruin of each, in consequence of that unfavourable balance of trade, which, they pretend, would be the infallible effect of an unrestrained commerce with the other" (*WN,* 4.3c.13, 496; emphasis added). When international traders' exhortations win the ear of politicians who shape policy, it bodes ill, Smith thinks, for productivity and long-term prosperity at home. Instead of promoting national wealth and economic growth and development, policies based on the balance of trade doctrine usually create artificially high profits in a chosen industry and discourage investment and productivity in others—perhaps ones more naturally deserving of the home country's focus. Smith thus presses home the point that traders' predictions are absurd—and perhaps knowingly false. As he comments in *Lectures on Jurisprudence,* no one has yet heard of a country ruined by being on the losing end of a balance of trade, even as it is figured in public debates as a potential catastrophe and a major risk to the country's prosperity and standing.

But the doctrine's absurdity and inaccuracy aside, Smith is particularly concerned by how and to what end it became "political maxim." He traces its birth to the widespread propensity for monopoly, arguing that "it was the spirit of monopoly which originally both invented and propagated this doctrine . . . and they who first taught it were by no means such fools as they who believed it. In every country it always is and must be the interest of the great body of the people to buy whatever they want of those who sell it cheapest." He emphasizes that the latter claim about the well-being of consumers is so obvious that it might have guided commercial practices and dispositions, "had not the interested sophistry of merchants and manufacturers confounded the common sense of mankind. Their interest is, in this respect, directly *opposite* to that of the great body of the people" (*WN,* 4.3c.10, 493–94). Smith is now tracing how an irresponsible approach to the risks of trade has produced political corruption. Particular groups of economic actors are now operating as particularly worrisome *political* actors—ones who work to shape political practice and policy to serve the purpose of shielding themselves from the downsides of commercial risk, at the expense of the common interest.

Smith thus pushes further than Hume in emphasizing that while the economic policies of the mercantile system, such as the balance of trade doctrine, are inefficient and perhaps shortsighted, it is more troubling that the *political* aspects of the mercantile system have simultaneously become so corrupt. He holds traders to account not only as a group of irresponsible commercial risk takers, but as a corrupt political class.

Smith also criticizes the statesmen who bend to the interests of influential and vocal international traders. He suggests, too, that the politician is also unable to brook the risks of a political career, and so he is vulnerable to outside influence in the worst way. The politician is, for Smith, "an insidious and crafty animal . . . whose councils are directed by the momentary fluctuations of affairs," and his account of mercantilist politics in *The Wealth of Nations* is in part a narrative about political privilege and the manipulation of political order to confront the inherent risk and flux of trade (*WN*, 4.2.39, 468). Rather than patiently bear with the vicissitudes of trade and the corresponding shifts in political climate, both traders and politicians attempt to control and redirect the entire system of political economy for gain. That is, by jettisoning, redistributing, or deferring losses, they try to discipline and govern risky ventures into schemes that only yield profit, rather than confront prudently the dual nature of risk. The consequences are borne by many, but especially by the public.

In noting the opposition of merchant interest to the public interest, Smith captures a politically and morally serious problem. The trouble is not only that the practice of trading has apparently produced a culture of men who are known for "mean rapacity," "impertinent jealousy," and monopolistic tendencies (*WN*, 4.3c.2, 9). An additional problem, which Smith emphasizes in a much sharper way than Hume does, is that when trade became national business, merchants became influential figures in politics—ones capable, as experts in trade, of influencing how heads of state and their publics view commercial relations with their neighbors. These merchants direct arguments in favor of monopoly and against unfavorable trade balances to "parliaments, and to councils of princes, to nobles and to country gentlemen: by those who were supposed to understand trade, to those who were conscious to themselves that they knew nothing about the matter" (*WN*, 4.1.10, 434).[12] Merchants' search to secure profit and deflect loss has thus, over time, pervaded politics, and as a result, "the meanness of merchant cultures [has] spilled over into the arena of national politics."[13] Consequently, "nations have been taught that their interest consisted in beggaring all their neighbours" (*WN*, 4.3c.9, 493). When statesmen adopt merchants' perspective on the risks of trade, they also create a potentially dangerous international climate for their nation-states, by failing to cultivate a culture of trust and credit with fellow trading states. Thus, when traders are consulted on or influence their home state's economic policy, they may effectively produce quite risky international politics.[14] At home, states that bend to the interests of traders ultimately fail to meet the domestic needs and interests of their publics (*WN*, 4.introduction, 428). In the introduction to book 4 of *Wealth of Nations*, Smith notes that the objects of political economy are to provide revenue and subsistence for the public and to garner enough public revenue to be able to provide services for the people. The rest of the book makes the case that the frequent collusion of traders, manufacturers, and statesmen ultimately undermines these two projects.

Smith's analysis thus sweeps out from his attention to the attitudes of individual risk takers in the political economy to include much more. His well-known critique of monopoly contains a deep criticism of the merchant *class* as a band of moral hazard actors who want only profit without being willing to shoulder losses, which they work to achieve through the creation of formal institutions like joint-stock companies or by overt political maneuvering to recast their specific interests, and their irresponsible confrontations with risk, as a public good. These policies and institutions, in turn, propagate the same lopsided perspective on risk that occasioned their founding. While the undesirable economic outcomes of the political maneuvering of producers, traders, and statesmen should catch his readers' attention, Smith persistently emphasizes that the real underlying problem—the move to squeeze profit out of risk-taking ventures without being vulnerable to any kind of loss—deserves readers' moral reprobation.

"Crushing These Adventurous Spirits": *Bentham and Smith on Usury and Risk*

Thus far I have argued that *The Wealth of Nations*, particularly its critique of monopolistic policies and structures in eighteenth-century British political economy, may be read as a sustained engagement with harmful attempts to govern risk. Smith begins with an exploration of the individual propensity to overvalue hope of success in the face of risk, and continues to an indictment of the merchant class as bent on exploiting risk through political means. While Smith's moral, political, and economic critique of bad risk taking is extremely ambitious in scope, his own vision of the proper confrontation with risk is, I argue, quite modest and highly individualized. To explore this, turn back to the individual as a source of hope for Smith, we must move away from his consideration of collective approaches to mitigating and confronting risk through institutions and efforts to control policy. By reading *A Defence of Usury,* Jeremy Bentham's 1787 critique of Smith's views on lending and interest in *The Wealth of Nations,* alongside Smith's account of prudence in the 1790 revisions to *The Theory of Moral Sentiments,* we find a return to Smith's initial unit of analysis, the risk-taking individual, who is something of a hero to Bentham and a persistent worry for Smith. Bentham's engagement with Smith on interest and risk throws into relief Smith's attention to the individual commercial actor, who can pose a problem for or a solution to the challenges of the inevitable confrontation with risk in political economy.

In *The Wealth of Nations,* Smith ponders the dangers of raising the national interest rate. He makes the following plea to keep interest low, a position rooted in his understanding of potentially harmful orientations to risk:

> The legal rate, it is to be observed, though it ought to be somewhat above, ought not to be much above the lowest market rate. If the legal rate of interest in Great Britain, for example, was fixed so high as eight or ten per cent, the greater part of the money which was to be lent, would be lent to *prodigals and projectors,* who alone would be willing to give this high interest. Sober people, who will give for the use of money no more than a part of what they are likely to make by the use of it, would not venture into the competition. A great part of the capital of the country would thus be kept out of the *hands* which were most likely to make a profitable *and* advantageous use of it, *and* thrown into those which were most likely to waste *and* destroy it. (*WN,* 2.4.16–17)

Here Smith takes pains to keep capital with those who would invest it carefully and grow it slowly. His claim here is that prudent commercial actors, in the same vein as the small proprietors or landowners who serve as the staid backbone of the political economy, would never risk borrowing at high rates, because of their keen respect for the downsides of such a risk. Instead, if interest rates were raised, lenders would have to cope with an influx of "prodigals and projectors," those with contempt for risk, who would recklessly borrow with no thought for the future. The only difference between these two types of undesirable commercial actors, Smith implies, is that prodigals would immediately squander the money, whereas projectors would invest in schemes likely to fail. But, the outcome is the same—raising the national interest would only infuse the political economy with even more unwanted risky behavior.

This particular passage in *The Wealth of Nations* caught the eye of Bentham, who, in an extremely jocular response to Smith, offered a different perspective on usury and risk. While Bentham sides with Smith on the problem of "prodigals," in *A Defence of Usury* he praises "projectors" against Smith, and by extension proposes a different view on the problem of risk in commercial Britain. As he writes to Smith:

> If I presume to contend with you, it is only in defence of what I look upon as, not only an innocent, but a most *meritorious* race of men, who are so unfortunate as to have fallen under the rod of your displeasure. I mean *projectors:* under which invidious name I understand you to comprehend, in particular, all such persons as, in the pursuit of wealth, strike out into any new channel, and more especially into any channel of invention.
>
> It is with the professed view of checking, or rather of crushing, these *adventurous spirits*, whom you rank with "prodigals", that you approve of the laws which limit the rate of interest, grounding yourself on the tendency, they appear to you to have, to keep the capital of the country out of two such different sets of hands.[15]

Here Bentham distinguishes projectors as a class of commercial actors worth admiring, people whose risk taking and penchant for exploring new "channels" and generating novel inventions offer something worthwhile to the political economy. He complains that it is unfair for them to bear the taint of disapprobation or for their efforts to be judged as "rashness, and folly, and absurdity, and knavery, and waste" instead of as a positive contribution.[16] For Bentham, "prudent projectors" are men to be encouraged and supported, as they are the ones who bring novelty to commercial society—they invent new things, establish and cultivate new arts, and generally set their minds to developing new ways to improve and ease the way for others. As he argues, many of the most appreciated, well-established goods were once inventions and novelties, too, and they had to be tried and tested by some bold projector. Bentham claims that putting money in the hands of these men is worth the risk—that is, it is worth the potential disappointment and loss that might result, if only because it might also bring novelty, gain, and progress to society.

While Bentham argues that the tradeoff Smith refuses to brook may be worth making, he still stresses that the risk of lending money to projectors is low. Because those who seek to fund novel projects are typically clever, industrious, and prudent in the way Smith himself praises some commercial actors in *The Wealth of Nations*, they generally meet with some success, although sometimes this success is evident only in hindsight. Bentham points out that Smith knows as much, since his own narrative of the progress of opulence in *The Wealth of Nations* is peppered with mentions of projects that did not end in ruin or waste. Bentham writes:

> I hope you may by this time be disposed to allow me that we have not been ill served by the projects of time past. I have already intimated, that I could not see any reason why we should apprehend our being worse served by the projects of time future. I will now venture to add, that I think I do see reason, why we should expect to be still better and better served by these projects, than by those. I mean better upon the whole, in virtue of the reduction which experience, if experience be worth any thing, should make in the proportion of the number of the ill-grounded and unsuccessful, to that of the well-grounded and successful ones.[17]

Bentham suggests here that breaking the wave of projectors seeking capital by lowering the rate of interest, a move that Smith advocates, is too cautious an approach. He argues that Smith wants to curb a risk that actually poses more upsides than drawbacks. Bentham faces the uncertain future with confidence in the endeavors of creative individuals, whom he thinks are the bearers of progress, at least "upon the whole" and over the long term.

Bentham's challenge to Smith introduces a countervailing orientation to risk taking in political economy, suggesting that risk gives civilization cause for hope rather than anxiety. In this sense, he counters Smith's grave pessimism about the human orientation to risk—a pessimism grounded in empirical observations of the economic practices and policies of mercantile Britain—with a perspective closer to Hume's. Bentham's is not a foolish optimism in the face of the unknown, but is instead a calculated appraisal of a future in which some risky and novel projects are likely to pan out and improve the conditions of humanity, if the future is to be anything like the past. Bentham does not tell a story in which risk poses no loss or in which the possibility of loss is recklessly ignored. Instead, he speculates that risky ventures may produce some desired good *over time*, even if losses come along the way. As such, he suggests against Smith that certain kinds of risk taking and risk takers are rightly valorized, and that societies should take a more hopeful outlook regarding these daring individuals and their endeavors.

Risk, Prudence, and Self-Command in The Theory of Moral Sentiments

Three years after Bentham's challenge, Smith returns to the question of the moral psychology and practices of economic actors that he first engaged in *The Wealth of Nations*, where his analysis prompted Bentham to reach out to him and insist that particular kinds of risk takers were essential to the progress of a commercial society. In a late revision to the last edition of *The Theory of Moral Sentiments*, published in 1790, Smith provides a new and sustained portrayal of the psychology of economic activity. Here he offers a normative reflection on the character of the commercial actor who seeks approbation, and he also argues for prudence as a critical economic virtue. In so doing, Smith may be formulating an antidote for the pathologies he diagnosed in eighteenth-century British politics and economy. He closely examines the role of the individual economic actor in a society saturated by risk, albeit a strongly socialized actor with deep ties to others.

In *The Theory of Moral Sentiments'* discussion of prudence, Smith situates his analysis of the pursuit of personal fortune in the context of the text's broad account of the human desire for social approbation. External fortune is, he notes, one of the most powerful sources of credit and esteem in society. In fact, one of the primary reasons people seek and acquire assets beyond what they need is to earn the admiration and approval of others. After explaining the psychological motives for the acquisition of wealth, Smith strongly suggests that the pursuit and maintenance of fortune—and the rank and reputation that go hand in hand with fortune—should largely boil down to a single moral virtue: prudence in the face of risk. He conceptualizes prudence largely in commercial terms, linking it to the careful protection of assets and the habits and activities of economic actors he had already praised in *The Wealth of Nations*.[18]

Smith's description of prudence and the skills and temperament of a prudent person primarily emphasizes the security-seeking tendencies of human beings in a commercial context. Prudence is not merely a matter of choosing the right action at the appropriate time, based on experience. Rather, it is a cautious virtue, "averse to expos[ing] our health, our fortune, our rank, or reputation to any sort of hazard." Smith writes that prudence is "rather cautious than enterprising, and more anxious to preserve the advantages which we already possess, than forward to prompt us to the acquisition of still greater advantages" (*TMS*, 6.1.6, 249). In other words, to be prudent is to be fundamentally respectful of both sides of risk, and the skills and practices of prudent people stem from their inclination to secure what they already have against the whims of chance, in stark contrast to the kinds of individuals who gave Smith pause in *The Wealth of Nations*.[19]

The character sketch of the prudent man is Smith's promotion of one approach to risk, arguably what he takes to be the proper orientation. The prudent actor is not one controlled by *fear* of venturing out into the choppy waters of business and exchange. Rather, he is a person of measured action; prudence motivates thoughtfulness and skill in economic endeavors, guiding economic actors to take some chances and to avoid others. As Smith writes, prudence drives people to avoid loss and hazard not merely by "frugality" and "parsimony," but also by "real knowledge and skill in . . . trade or profession" and "assiduity and industry in the exercise of it" (*TMS*, 6.1.6, 250). Any new ventures and chosen risks the prudent person takes in the political economy are not rashly decided, but are instead the products of preparation and calculation of probable success or failure, consistent with the prudent economic actor's character:

> He has no anxiety to change so comfortable a situation, and does not go in quest of new enterprises and adventures, which might endanger but could not well increase, the secure tranquility which he actually enjoys. If he enters into any new projects or enterprises, they are likely to be well concerted and well prepared. He can never be hurried or drove into them by any necessity, but has always time and leisure to deliberate soberly and coolly concerning what are likely to be their consequences. (*TMS*, 6.1.12, 252)

Thus the prudent individual displays Smithian self-command in a realm of shifting and enticing economic opportunities. He weighs probable outcomes very carefully before acting and tends to behave conservatively when it comes to risk taking. The prudent man's perspective on risk is that it largely poses a strong hazard of loss, a possibility that is always foremost in his mind and may consistently trump a countervailing hope of gain. But it is critical to note that he is not paralyzed by his anxiety, even though he is slow to take chances. Nor does he attempt to evade the consequences of risks badly chosen.

Smith also explores a second dimension of the prudent man's reserved character and penchant for control, which was also featured in *The Wealth of Nation's* critique of the mercantile system. The prudent person generally eschews social and political paths to economic prosperity, preferring to restrict himself to purely commercial endeavors. Smith comments that he builds not only his fortune but also his reputation on his store of professional knowledge and skill, instead of by currying favor with those "little clubs and cabals" whose machinations shape commercial policy (*TMS*, 6.1.7, 250). To this end, while friendly and honorable in his dealings with others, he is somewhat asocial. He steers clear of associations that might "interfere with the regularity of his temperance, interrupt the steadiness of his industry, or break in upon the strictness of his frugality" (*TMS*, 6.1.9, 251). Moreover, he avoids politics almost entirely, focusing on his own private affairs. Smith notes that a prudent person will never decline public service if asked, but "he will not cabal in order to force himself into it," as he would rather leave this work to others (*TMS*, 6.1.13, 253). As such, the prudent commercial actor is self-reliant, although keen to win the approbation of others through displays of expertise, self-command, and credit-worthy character. Prudence, while not terribly heroic as far as moral virtues go, is the most reliable guide to capital accumulation and the subsequent social esteem that Smith thinks everyone wants. And it also provides a significant counterweight to the kinds of impulses and practices that Smith deems so pathological in *The Wealth of Nations*.

The sketch of the prudent economic actor offered here is not meant to argue that radical asociality and myopia regarding fortune are the bedrock of a flourishing commercial society or even the key to a happy life.[20] Rather, we should interpret *The Theory of Moral Sentiments'* brief moral reflection on economic prudence as a depiction of what Smith takes to be the proper orientation to economic risk taking. That is, Smith urges caution, careful reasoning, and choice when it comes to risk, although there seems to be no place for paralyzing fear in his depiction of political economy.

Smith's emphasis on prudence as a significant economic virtue in the 1790 edition of *The Theory of Moral Sentiments* distills powerfully his scattered observations on the character and practices of commercial actors in *The Wealth of Nations*. The catalog of economic behavior and the depiction of the psychology of economic activity is much more varied in the latter text. In *The Wealth of Nations*, Smith tracks different kinds of behavior and various orientations to risk, many of them highly imprudent when viewed through the interpretive grid offered by the account of prudence that appears later in *The Theory of Moral Sentiments*. But, the intersection of Smith's two major works on the question of prudence brings out two critical points. First is Smith's care to establish parsimony and caution as the norm for actors who seek to better their conditions—these characteristics must discipline, or at least exist alongside, the potentially costly pursuit of novel industry and trade. As Smith asserts in *The Wealth of Nations*, "parsimony, and not industry, is the immediate cause of the increase of capital." More pointedly, he also notes that "prodigality and misconduct" deplete capital (*WN*, 2.3.16, 337). The proper response to the allure of risk—and Smith keenly perceives the psychological and economic appeal of risk taking for many people—is to proceed with caution, either saving what one has instead of investing in new endeavors or reserving at least a substantial portion to offset the dangers of undertaking new and uncertain enterprises. Certainly, his views on prudence in *The Theory of Moral Sentiments* also support the idea that caution and thrift, rather than boldness and whimsy, are to be preferred in a commercial society.

Second, and related, is Smith's emphasis on individuals' hard-earned expertise and skill over political or "publick" routes to the maintenance of fortune. He insists that individuals must reflect on their skills and abilities, as well as other variables, and attempt to discern whether economic risk taking is likely to be profitable. What they must not do, however, is proceed blindly on a whim and then secure themselves against undesirable outcomes via political influence or channels.

Smith's return to the individual economic actor and to the private virtue of prudence is a quite modest intervention in the early modern debate regarding how risk ought to be managed. It is true to his critique of mercantilism, an account of a system distorted by the ambitions and schemes of powerful commercial actors who will not accept the losses entailed by their experimentation with risk, and those of the politicians whose interests are tied to these actors' economic power. That Smith would be critical of such a system is no surprise—in addition to his economic and political attack on the system-distorting efforts of traders and their political bedfellows, he would likely object on epistemological grounds as well.

Smith's epistemological commitments should bring him, and his readers, back to more modest considerations of how an individual might cultivate the kind of character that would resist the dangerous appeal of risk.

Modesty in the Face of Risk: Smith on Epistemology and System

In the last revisions of *The Theory of Moral Sentiments*, Smith offers a brief but sharp criticism of "the man of system," who is moved to impose broad political reform by the aesthetic appeal of his own well-ordered ideal plan for society. The trouble lies, according to Smith, with the man's faulty perception of both the society to be reordered and its constituent members. As he puts it, the man of system

> seems to imagine that he can arrange the different members of a great society with as much ease as the hand arranges the different pieces upon a chess–board. He does not consider that the pieces upon the chess–board have no other principle of motion besides that which the hand impresses upon them; but that, in the great chess–board of human society, every single piece has a principle of motion of its own. (*TMS*, 6.2.17, 275)

Whether or not these "pieces" abide by the same principle that drives the proposed reform is a matter of chance. If they do, social life will proceed smoothly, and if they do not, then society is bound to be disrupted, probably for the worse.

Smith's treatment of the man of system, while offered as a critique of radical constitutional reform, also sheds some light on what splits more prudential economic actors from imprudent and vicious ones.[21] And it pairs well with the problem of risk, as risk management is essentially bound up with the question of how well people can imagine the scope and possibilities of the future. Smith's comments on the man of system suggest that efforts to confront risk must take place on a small scale, in the activities of the prudent. As he has explained, prudent individuals cope with the inherent risks of commercial activity by means under their direct control, building incremental knowledge of the trends and background conditions of their fields and practicing good habits of order and economy, so as to present themselves as exchange partners worthy of the trust and credit that can mediate risk. Their efforts to study their economic conditions with care are paired always with cultivating a cautious and reflective character. Even traders, who are perhaps imprudent in their choice of work, as *The Wealth of Nations* implies, can still be moderate and prudent in their pursuit of profit via trade, remaining attuned to both the profits and losses endemic to risky ventures, but avoiding the extremes of an overly presumptuous or excessively fearful perspective on risk taking. Second, in Smith's bold critique of abusive and negligent corporate management, manipulation of the flow of trade at home and abroad, and aggressive pursuit of political clout, he is exploring the figure of the trader as a second kind of problematic commercial actor. Here, the trader is a kind of "man of system," who attempts to rework economic and political order to his own ends of capital accumulation with no chance of loss, in tandem with his fellow traders.

Smith's conception of order, which rests on an acceptance of uncertainty, anticipates that risk will be part of any system of political economy. The enthusiasm of this second, corrupt order of traders for risk's profit potential, buttressed by constant political maneuvering to displace or defer loss, ultimately distorts the entire system in ways that Smith notices and condemns. Worse still is the corrupting effect these practices have on the moral economy. In the end, Smith zeroes in on a different kind of hubris related to risk than the one he initially diagnoses. Although he asserts time and again that traders, the animating figures of commercial society, are excessively confident that risky ventures will pay off, his analysis of the pathologies of mercantilist politics suggests this most prominent class of commercial actors may actually be too immodest about their ability to jettison all loss.

CHAPTER SIX

AN AGE OF RISK,
A LIBERALISM OF ANXIETY

I n Michel Foucault's late lectures on liberal governmentality, he suggests that the problems of danger and persistent crisis constitute liberalism, or the "liberal art of government." He asserts

> that the motto of liberalism is: "Live dangerously." "Live dangerously," that is to say, individuals are constantly exposed to danger, or rather, they are conditioned to experience their situation, their life, their present, and their future as containing danger. I think this kind of stimulus of danger will be one of the major implications of liberalism ... everywhere you see this stimulation of the fear of danger which is, as it were, the condition, the internal psychological and cultural correlative of liberalism. There is no liberalism without a culture of danger.[1]

Liberal governance must, Foucault argues, perpetually address the interests of political subjects by exacting a careful balance between security and freedom to protect the community from dangers, both real and imagined. He suggests that we should look to the nineteenth century to find evidence for this turn to a liberalism of "living dangerously." The nineteenth century witnessed a series of campaigns meant to stimulate and soothe simultaneously a sense of impending danger in political subjects—broad efforts to promote hygiene and disease prevention, the rise of crime journalism and crime fiction, and campaigns for savings banks to help people prepare for economic crises.[2] Foucault tracks how liberalism fuses practices of discipline and control with the production and consumption of a host of individual freedoms, arguing that liberalism's tension between freedom and security finds its roots in a culture of danger.

I argue in this book that by the end of the eighteenth century, a culture of persistent anxiety was already present in early modern Britain, and that this anxiety is traceable to the challenges of negotiating a new world understood not in terms danger but through the lens of Janus-faced risk. Preoccupation with uncertainty, a view of risk as hazard, and profound feelings of insecurity marked eighteenth-century efforts to understand the present and imagine the future. While this perspective, which frequently elides the difference between risk and loss, would go on to find firmer footing in the nineteenth century, it gained a toehold in the eighteenth century, as shown by work on probability, risk, and political economy.

Liberalism's entanglement with a culture of fear and worry may thus well begin even further back than Foucault allows.[3] I would argue that what he is describing comes less from "living dangerously" and more from living with risk. Eighteenth-century thinkers like Hume and Smith describe and theorize deeply socialized individuals struggling to negotiate the dual character of risk, to accept all at once the opportunities it offers and the losses it threatens. Readers of Smith and Hume cannot help but notice that in these theorists' representations of how people imagine and live with risk, one side of the story about risk wins out. Commercial society, as Smith and Hume figure it, is populated by people who zero in on the darker or threatening aspects of risk, who feel deeply the anxieties that come with thinking about the future probabilistically, and who make a variety of pathological choices in a risk-laden political economy. These choices are traceable to people's refusal to embrace both sides of risk simultaneously, to think through the full range of possible consequences of risky ventures, and to manage their affairs accordingly.

If we are looking at the emergence of a liberalism premised on the interplay among risk, fear, and anxiety, as I think we are, then perhaps it is fitting that my account of the development of risk and the subsequent confrontations with its possibilities and perils in early modern Britain ends with Smith's 1790 reflections on the potential that lies with a certain kind of individual. The prudent man is, for Smith, a rare figure of prudence and self-command in a risk-laden commercial society. Prudence, a combination of realistic caution, calculation, and intellectual modesty in the face of the risky opportunities in a commercial political economy, is a highly individualized solution to what Smith diagnoses as a large-scale systemic problem in mercantile Britain—an approach to commercial risk that is guided by a strange combination of fear and hubris.

Smith's is perhaps the most sweeping eighteenth-century critique of efforts to manage and exploit risk, but the solution he offers can only work slowly and on the smallest scale. This solution is in keeping Smith's own resistance to radical transformations of existing systems, a core feature of his liberalism. By the time Smith writes about risk, it is a permanent feature of commercial political economy and a problem for everyone, but he suggests that it might yet be managed well, through the cultivation of virtuous character among those who must confront it. For Smith, a commercial society of risk composed of these sorts of individuals might have a chance to be prosperous, ethical, and self-regulating, protected by the rule of law and supported by prudent policies. This is a modest intervention but a potentially powerful one; a clear-eyed perspective on risk taking and its potential consequences—perilous or promising—at the individual level might well lead to better decisions and institutional transformation over time.

But, as I have argued, the emergence of risk and debates about its management in early modern Britain began somewhere much more audacious than where Smith leaves us—in the 1650s with Hobbes's radical call for a transformative civil science that can eradicate uncertainty (and by extension, risk) from politics altogether. For Hobbes, uncertainty cannot really be governed or managed successfully, but instead must be displaced. Hobbes's intervention—so different in tone and scale from Smith's—begins an important conversation on uncertainty, risk, and politics in early modern British political thought, but his efforts to marry certain knowledge with secure politics cannot settle definitively the important questions that he raises. His confrontation with the pain of uncertainty and his efforts to displace it with a geometric approach to acquiring certain knowledge of politics appear simply to force a return to older, prudential, and much less stable forms of experiential knowledge as a better way forward in politics and economy—the very forms he criticizes.

In much of my source material for this account of the significance of risk for early modern British political and economic thought, the turn to prudence and probability shows in early form what we still believe to be true today: that risk and uncertainty are simply constituent parts of our experiences as social, political, and economic actors, and that while we may cope with them using more or less sophisticated forms of knowledge, we cannot remove them from the human condition. Unfortunately, this turn also occasions the cultivation of a culture of anxiety that still haunts us today, and the search for ways to soothe ourselves is still ongoing.

CHAPTER SIX

In the introduction to this book, I suggest that a study of risk in early modern Britain yields three insights that persist in importance for those of us concerned about the problem of risk in the twenty-first century. There I note that risk discourse is dominated by two particular narratives about what risk is—either an opportunity for profit and the exercise of freedom and agency, or a threat to security and a problem to be solved. I argue that it is important to recognize that risk poses both possibilities at once, frequently leaving it to those taking or exposed to risks to negotiate risk's dual character and the ensuing passions of hope and fear. But, as this study has shown, by the end of the eighteenth century, when risk had really taken hold as a permanent problem for commercial societies, the scales seem to have tipped in favor of the view that all risks are more threatening than they are promising. Hume's work is instructive here, for thinking about the future in terms of risk as tantamount to experiencing blind uncertainty and its attendant fears marks a turn to depicting the risk-taking subject as a predominantly fearful one. Even Smith's work, which emphasizes the problem of heedless optimism among those economic actors who take the boldest risks, ultimately reveals a system warped by the efforts of traders and politicians who take suspect measures to cope with the anxieties provoked by the risks of their professions. Perhaps this is the point to suggest that we often conflate risk with another of its companion concepts—danger—and fail to recognize that even the most threatening risky endeavors may bear the promise of profit for someone. In many respects, at the end of the eighteenth century, we find ourselves where Hobbes left us in the 1650s and where Foucault finds us in the nineteenth century—with an account of political subjectivity constituted by deep fear of the unknown.

This emergence of a fearful, anxious risk-taking subject relates very closely to an important knowledge problem in early modern engagements with risk. While theoretically we *can* know the difference between uncertainty and risk, in practice we often have real difficulty parsing the two, an experiential phenomenon that exacerbates our anxieties about the future and makes decision making particularly taxing. My book follows the emergence of philosophical probability as a critical tool for addressing the perpetual challenge for all human communities—vulnerability in the face of a future that is fundamentally unknowable. Probability is thus a way forward, and one that receives attention and detail. But as I show in my interpretations of the works of Hobbes, Locke, and Hume, uncertainty still holds a significant place in early modern thinking about risk. Uncertainty shapes and conditions accounts of human community, thought, and action. It is *the* problem that Hobbes sets out to solve in the interest of a peaceful, secure politics; it is a basic fact to be accepted about the political world for Locke; and for Hume, it is the source of healthy skepticism as well as deep anxiety for those who try to act in the social, political, and economic world.

The thinkers in this study who accept uncertainty are also, I argue, the ones who are able to embrace and develop a notion of risk as central to politics and political economy. This should not be surprising, as risk is intimately connected to probabilistic thinking, which is by definition a form of knowledge that can only be more or less, but never wholly, certain. Locke's turn to probabilistic thinking as a crucial political tool for both a people and the government to which it entrusts its well-being makes him an early thinker of risk. For Locke, as probability cuts through the morass of blind uncertainty to help political actors speculate about the future, politics becomes an arena of risk. Likewise, Hume's detailed taxonomy of probability is nothing if not a description of how people think about the risks an uncertain future might hold, and more importantly, what kinds of affective responses the process of thinking probabilistically triggers.

One helpful feature of Hume's analysis of risk is that he captures a serious problem emphasized by later thinkers of uncertainty and risk, such as the twentieth-century economist Frank Knight. The Knightian "fatal ambiguity" that hounds efforts to parse risk and uncertainty is theorized in early form in Hume's *Treatise* and in his other writings on probability. Because Hume understands this ambiguity in judgment, he is also able to grasp why thinking about the future largely triggers fear, anxiety, and dread in people. And unfortunately, this is true whether we think probabilistically and calculate future outcomes with some precision, or simply face the future with blind uncertainty. As Hume notices, calculating a probable future and staring into the void feel the same, and they stir the same passions, ones that are difficult to bear. Hume's analysis thus suggests that we will continue to have difficulty overcoming the "fatal ambiguity" in our own judgment that runs together uncertainty and risk. As our methods for calculating risk become more sophisticated and our data about the past and present more comprehensive, we may be able to predict oncoming risks with more precision and be able to think more creatively about how to confront them. But if Hume is right, this will not be a soothing enterprise, and if anything, it should make us more attuned to the daunting knowledge that we live daily with uncertainty.[4]

To end on a slightly more sanguine note, while this book tracks the challenges and possibilities of governing the fearful, risk-averse subject that emerges from an early modern engagement with the problem of risk, it also finds resources for this project. Early modern thinkers conclude that stable networks, relationships, and practices of trust and credit might offer avenues forward. Trust becomes of keen significance to societies that find themselves saturated by risk, even as trust produces risks of its own. I argue that we should reinterpret Locke's famed account of trust and politics such that it becomes clear what role risk has to play in a political community structured as a trust. For Locke, modeling political society on a fiduciary trust highlights the risks of mutual relationships of obligation and benefit. While trust is, on Locke's read, perhaps the most effective resource a people has for confronting the contingent and uncertain elements of politics, it poses a risk itself and must be scrutinized carefully as a potential source of loss and suffering. In Smith's descriptive account of mercantilist politics and political economy, we see such a difficult and undesirable case play out, in which purported experts in the field of trade violate norms of trust and credibility by acting recklessly in their commercial dealings and by working to offset their bad risk taking by capturing political power.

But in Hume's work, we find another approach, in which he attempts to draw on relations of trust between himself and his reading public by extending and moderating their knowledge of commerce to argue for a different orientation to the risks of political economy. That is, he urges his readers to confront the risks of trade with equanimity, patience, and fortitude, armed with some hope that the system of trade might produce profit if left to run its course. As such, he turns away from the liberal project of stimulating danger that Foucault envisions and toward a project of stimulating hope and relief.

NOTES

Chapter One: Introduction

1. Ewald, "Two Infinities of Risk," 226.
2. Niklas Luhmann wrote in 1993 that no one had done an etymological study or conceptual history of risk; the risk literature at that time had little more than brief nods to the etymological origins of risk as a medieval word with a specific meaning tied to maritime insurance. Luhmann, *Risk*, 9–11. Fortunately, this is no longer the case, as scholars are beginning to tell the history of risk as a concept and an important feature of everyday life. Elaine Freedgood's *Victorian Writing about Risk* interprets a broad range of popular literature to uncover how ordinary British citizens coped with both the dangerous and the exciting dimensions of risk. Most recently, Jonathan Levy has argued for the emergence of a modern idea of risk in the nineteenth century and has explained its implications for the institutions, behaviors, and norms of a newly capitalist America. Levy, *Freaks of Fortune*.
3. Levy notes that in the United States, it took until the early nineteenth century for "risk" to come loose from its specific origin as a form of marine insurance and mean something more general in ordinary usage. I argue here that this happened earlier in Britain, through a slow transformation in the late seventeenth and early eighteenth centuries. By the time Adam Smith was working out his account of political economy in the 1760s and 1770s, he was using risk to describe all manner of relationships, circumstances, and choices. Levy, *Freaks of Fortune*, 3.
4. Ian Hacking notes the appearance of French and Italian cognates of "risk" as early as the mid-sixteenth century and attributes these words to members of a commercial class. See Hacking, "Risk and Dirt," 25. Unlike most scholars, who offer brief sketches of the etymology of "risk," Fred Drucker traces the term "risk" to Arabic origins and translates it as "earning one's daily bread," also highlighting its

relationship to political economy. See Drucker, *The Practice of Management*, 46.

5. *OED Online*, s.v. "risk," accessed October 31, 2012, http://www.oed
    .com/view/Entry/166307. By the late seventeenth century, English-
    speaking people were also using "risk" as a transitive verb meaning
    "to endanger" or "to expose to the chance of injury, death, or loss."
    This is still the prevalent meaning of "risk."

6. Peter Bernstein tells us that the "revolutionary idea that defines the
    boundary between modern times and the past is the mastery of risk:
    the notion that the future is more than a whim of the gods and that
    men and women are not passive before nature." Bernstein, *Against
    the Gods*, 1. While I disagree with the claim that moderns were the
    first to overcome a passive unwillingness to confront an unknown fu-
    ture, I think Bernstein is right to note that of modernity's many proj-
    ects, conceiving the future in terms of risks to be mastered has been
    and continues to be central. And furthermore, I share the intuition
    that efforts to understand, think, and write about risk—as opposed
    to fate, chance, providence, or fortune—may have significantly al-
    tered the social, political, and economic landscape.

7. Much of the conceptual work on risk is from sociologists and social
    theorists, who underscore two main features of risk: First, risk is a
    category of understanding; that is, there is no risk without our knowl-
    edge of it, no risk before we think of it. Put another way, without a
    particular kind of cognitive activity—the assessment of the magni-
    tude and scope of potential outcomes—there is no risk. See espe-
    cially Garland, "The Rise of Risk," 52. Moreover, when subjected to
    calculation or estimation in this way, anything can become a risk.
    Second, though the literature varies on the question of how to cope
    with risk, it is organized by the common idea that risk is a perma-
    nent feature of social life, and therefore we must do *something* with
    it. This literature on risk is vast and has grown considerably since the
    groundbreaking work of Ulrich Beck. See Beck, *Risk Society* and *World
    Risk Society*. Along with Beck, two other major scholars of contempo-
    rary social theories of risk are Anthony Giddens and Luhmann. All
    three argue that risk is a feature of what Beck calls "advanced mo-
    dernity." See Giddens, *Modernity and Self-Identity*; and Luhmann, *Risk*.
    In political theory, discussions of risk appear most frequently in
    theories of governmentality, which try to explain transformations
    in power and rule in late modernity, especially in the twentieth cen-

tury. This work all refers in one way or another to Michel Foucault's 1978 lecture on governmentality. See Gordon, Burchell, and Miller, *The Foucault Effect*; Dean, *Governmentality*; and Franklin, "Politics and Risk." Foucault developed these ideas in his other lectures as well; see especially Foucault, *Security, Territory, Population*, and *The Birth of Biopolitics*.

8. Hacking, *The Emergence of Probability, The Taming of Chance*, and "Risk and Dirt"; Shapin, *A Social History of Truth*; Shapiro, *Probability and Certainty in Seventeenth-Century England*; and Van Leeuwen, *The Problem of Certainty in English Thought*.

9. Although contemporary social and political theorists, particularly those who work on security and governmentality, attend closely to the problem of risk, surprisingly little work has been done on how risk has been conceptualized in either canonical or ephemeral texts in the history of political thought. In a rare exception, David Runciman explores the role risk plays in contemporary British and American political policy and rhetoric, turning to Hobbes, Rousseau, and the Abbé Sieyès to illuminate issues and concerns pertaining to public perception. See Runciman, *The Politics of Good Intentions*. Interest in studying risk in historical perspective and across the humanities has grown in the last decade or so. See note 2, with references to Freedgood's and Levy's studies, which have broken ground on this new effort. There has long been, however, a thriving and coherent literature in the intellectual history of probability, which is so important to the history of risk. See, for example, Daston, *Classical Probability in the Enlightenment*; Douglas, *Risk and Blame*; Gigerenzer et al., *The Empire of Chance*; and Hacking, *The Emergence of Probability* and *The Taming of Chance*. Many of these texts consider the link between probability and risk.

10. As Garland notes, "Risk begins where certain knowledge ends. Claims about risk are, literally, *uncertain* knowledge claims—impressionistic guesses, informed estimates, and probabilistic predictions about a future that cannot fully be known." Garland, "The Rise of Risk," 52.

11. In late modern and contemporary risk discourse, the terms "risk" and "uncertainty" themselves hold what Frank Knight calls a "fatal ambiguity," such that we must be careful to associate risks with "measured uncertainties," which we can estimate with some precision, and uncertainty with those we cannot. Human judgment frequently conflates the two. Knight, *Risk, Uncertainty, and Profit*, 233.

Chapter Two: "Experience Concludeth Nothing Universally"

1. I cite Hobbes's work in the text using the following abbreviations:

   Behemoth is cited as *B*, followed by page number.

   De Cive is cited as *DC*, followed by chapter and paragraph number.

   De Corpore is cited as *DCo*, followed by book and chapter number.

   Elements of Law is cited as *EL*, followed by book, chapter, and paragraph number.

   Leviathan is cited as *L*, followed by chapter and paragraph number.

   The introductory material to Hobbes's translation of *The Peloponnesian War* is cited as *TPW*, followed by page number.

2. Admittedly, Hobbes himself does not use the word "risk" in his work on future-oriented epistemology or politics, although it would have been in circulation by the time he was working. To my knowledge, three references to "risk" appear in the notes to Hobbes's translation of Thucydides's *The History of the Peloponnesian War*, and these are comments from early editors who find that Hobbes's descriptions of danger or uncertainty are actually better captured by the word "risk." The word itself, however, does not appear to have been part of Hobbes's lexicon. Although this is a significant point to bear in mind, my argument in this chapter is that Hobbes's work still articulates the clear stakes of a struggle with uncertainty in politics. Moreover, he offers a careful consideration of how far prudential and experiential reasoning can serve political actors, set against other, more certain forms of political knowledge. Though his work does not produce a well-developed theoretical treatment of "risk" per se, I argue that he sets the theoretical components in place for the thinkers who follow him—uncertainty, prudence and predictive thought, and action.

3. For an account of prudence as a premodern virtue that helps people contend with contingencies, see especially Pocock, *The Machiavellian Moment*, 3–30.

4. J.G.A. Pocock situates Hobbes's discussion of experience and prudence as one of two options available to seventeenth-century thinkers, who were trying to cope with the problem of politics in time and any contingencies or emergencies that emerged. He notes that one option was the "rhetoric . . . of fortune and innovation, cycle

and equilibrium," as a way of explaining political instability and suggesting how it could be managed, but Hobbes rejects this option in favor of a discussion of ancient prudence, so that he might "reject or minimize" prudence later. Pocock, "Time, History, and Eschatology," 153.

5. Springborg, "Hobbes and Historiography," 44.

6. Cf. Beck, *World Risk Society*, 137.

7. This foreshadows one of the major insights of contemporary theories of risk: When we conceive of risks, we construct future possibilities, often with reference to a known past. We cannot seem to help but act once we have this knowledge, and in doing so we also change the world in which the perceived risk is situated, by either altering the risk itself or creating the potential for new ones. John Adams puts rather poetically that "risk perceived is risk acted upon. It changes in the twinkling of an eye as the eye lights upon it." Adams, *Risk*, 30. This temporal dimension of risk, and its relationship to uncertainty, gives rise to a major observation of the risk literature—that risk is permanent and ubiquitous, even as we try to manage it.

8. See Borot, "History in Hobbes' Thought"; Rogers, "Hobbes, History and Wisdom"; Schuhmann, "Hobbes' Concept of History"; and Springborg, "Hobbes and Historiography." For interpretations of *Behemoth* situated in the context of larger discussions of Hobbes's views on history and historians, see Ashcraft, "Ideology and Class in Hobbes' Political Theory"; and Kraynak, "Hobbes's *Behemoth* and the Argument for Absolutism."

9. Hobbes divides natural history from civil history; for him, natural history is the history of facts that do not result from man's will, and civil history is a record of the "deeds of men in commonwealths" (*L*, 9.1).

10. Scott, "The Peace of Silence," 112–36.

11. Hobbes's historical reflections are not confined to *Behemoth*, of course. As all readers notice, *Leviathan*, too, is full of historical examples, especially those gleaned from biblical history; how these stand in relation to what Hobbes is trying to demonstrate scientifically varies depending on the moment.

12. For an account of the controversy surrounding the possibilities of certainty in early modern mathematics, see especially Shapin, *A Social History of Truth*, ch. 7.

13. This is the point at which a touch of what we would call the economic perspective may enter Hobbes's analysis. Craig Muldrew argues convincingly that the political theory of *Leviathan* has much to say about

the social-economic character of transactions between individuals. Hobbes describes these exchanges as marked by practices of reckoning and promising, which find a clear parallel in trade and credit. Muldrew, *The Economy of Obligation*, ch. 6.

14. As Noel Malcolm comments, the "essential similarity" between Hobbes's civil science and geometry was "striking" if also a bit troubled:

> Both sciences yielded universal truths by pressing the connections between conceptual entities: lines, circles, and squares, or rights, duties, and laws. To express the relationship between the sovereign and the citizens was to expound an analytic truth, similar to that which states the relationship between a circle and its radii. Unfortunately, however, beyond this type of immediate similarity there lay a very shadowy terrain of uncertain resemblances and shifting implications. (Malcolm, *Aspects of Hobbes*, 152)

Malcolm also notes that these difficulties had two sources that were very particular to Hobbes's mathematical work—his shifting views on geometry itself and his practice of "playing down the peculiar status of the objects of geometry as conceptual entities." The latter is likely more troubling for Hobbes's effort to subject civil scientific inquiry to the geometric framework.

15. See also Mathiowetz, *Appeals to Interest*, ch. 4. Part of Mathiowetz's effort to interpret Hobbes as an anti-interest theorist is a critique of his attempt to impose a geometric on politics and its language.

16. Locke thought so, too, and hoped to apply the same kind of systematic demonstration to morality. But unlike Hobbes, he did not force the application and may have concluded that moral language is too arbitrary to be subjected to the geometer's methods of representing concepts and working out proofs. See Dawson, *Locke, Language, and Early Modern Philosophy*, 248–49.

17. Jeffrey Collins situates this text in particular as part of a broad political and ecclesiological dispute between Hobbes and a set of university men. See Collins, *The Allegiance of Thomas Hobbes*, 214–18. The impassioned tone of *Six Lessons*, along with other documents of the dispute, may ironically undermine Hobbes's claim that geometry is immune to conflict "because men care not, in that subject, what be truth, as a thing that crosses no man's ambition, profit, or lust" (*L*, 11.21).

18. Hobbes, *Six Lessons to the Professors of the Mathematiques*, 1. Emphasis added.

19. Interpreting Hobbes's view of how names are imposed is notoriously tricky. On the one hand, he may acknowledge that people name merely by convention. Using prudence as a guide, they decide collectively on terms and definitions and impose them thereafter. On the other hand, he also appears to think people can be more or less correct about words and their definitions, which suggests that he thinks definitions can be true or false, and that this is the case prior to conventional formulations. Moreover, it is not clear that these two positions are entirely incompatible for him, which makes it hard to sort out exactly how *he* imposes definitions. Philip Pettit captures this well, noting that "Hobbes continually innovates in the definitions of his own crucial terms, much to the chagrin of his contemporaries, and . . . he regularly claims novelty for the definitions he puts forward. In order to take him seriously, we must suppose that while he recognizes that his definitions are often new, he still thinks of them as cleaving more carefully to patterns of common usage. Or if not to actual common usage, at least to the patterns that common usage would assume in the absence of any influence from the mistaken definitions he rejects." Pettit, *Made with Words*, 41. For further discussion of this point see Jesseph, "Hobbes and the Method of Natural Science," 86–107. Cf. Strong, "How to Write Scripture."

20. Hobbes, *Six Lessons to the Professors of the Mathematiques*, 14.

21. Ibid., 9.

22. For discussion of seventeenth-century concerns with the artifice and construction of the commonwealth from the ground up, see especially the introduction in Kahn, *Wayward Contracts*.

23. Hobbes makes this point in the introduction, where arguably he is addressing a sovereign, as I discuss later. Still, the plea could really address any reader, if Hobbes is correct about human beings and about the inherently democratic aspects of geometry:

> He that is to govern a whole nation, must read in himself, not this or that particular man; but mankind: which though it be hard to do, harder than to learn any language or science; yet when I shall have set down my own reading orderly, and perspicuously, the pains left another, will be only to consider, if he also find not the same in himself. For this kind of doctrine admitteth no other demonstration. (*L*, introduction.4)

24. Hobbes scholars have long disagreed over how to interpret what work fear of death does for Hobbes's political theory. For an account of fear

of death as the key passion that promotes reason-based approaches to politics, see Strauss, *The Political Philosophy of Hobbes*. For rational-choice arguments that Hobbes's claim about us fearing violent death is strictly a normative one, see Gauthier, *The Logic of Leviathan*; and Hampton, *Hobbes and the Social Contract Tradition*. Richard Tuck's claim is more nuanced; he thinks that self-preservation is a good candidate for a foundational principle of politics, because even if we do not always fear death, we can at least find it understandable when others do whatever it takes to avoid death. See Tuck, "Hobbes' Moral Philosophy." Victoria Kahn makes a critique of all these approaches; she argues that Hobbes's political project depends on a contract with his readers based on acceptance of his account of passions (including fear and its objects) and imagination. See Kahn, "Hobbes, Romance, and the Contract of Mimesis."

25. For an argument about the social character of knowledge, as Hobbes conceives it, see especially the concluding chapter of Schaffer and Shapin, *Leviathan and the Air-Pump*.

26. This is not to assert that Hobbes desires a scientific community of experts who work behind closed doors. If anything, he favors geometry in particular because its practices are conducive to publicity and less politicized than other intellectual pursuits, like scholastic philosophy or theology. The only criteria for the man of civil science seem to be curiosity, leisure, and the right method (*L*, 30.19). There is thus at least a democratic flavor to Hobbes's science, if not to his commonwealth itself.

27. For Tuck, this is the sticking point of Hobbes's theory—his aspirations were for citizens to really transform themselves, to shake off the passions that stood between them and political peace, by authorizing sovereign power. What I am arguing here is compatible, I think, with Tuck's view; I argue that citizens must assent to both Hobbes's description of them, to the model of politics that he thinks will best manage their passions, and to the practical manifestation of that model in the person of the sovereign. Tuck reads this as radical and utopian, and I think this chapter also expresses that view, but from a different angle. Tuck, "The Utopianism of *Leviathan*," 125–38.

28. See, for example, Schaffer and Shapin, *Leviathan and the Air-Pump*; Jesseph, *Squaring the Circle*; Malcolm, *Aspects of Hobbes*; and Collins, *The Allegiance of Thomas Hobbes*.

29. Here I focus mostly on whether the alliance between civil science and sovereign power is fragile, and whether experience and prudence

are also required for political decision making, in keeping with the concerns of this chapter. Arash Abizadeh argues convincingly that sovereign power, as Hobbes designs it, is meant to be inherently fragile and illusory. Further, its illusory nature is stressed by Hobbes as a means of reinforcing sovereign power, by reminding readers how close they always are to living without order. Abizadeh, "The Representation of Hobbesian Sovereignty," 113–52.

30. Hobbes also suggests that in addition to direct experience, counselors will have to sift through and interpret records of fact from the commonwealth's archives—everything from treaties to correspondence. This is interpretive work, not unlike what the historian does (*L*, 25.14).

31. A second example, and perhaps an even more troubling one for Hobbes, is the discussion in *Leviathan* 21 concerning conscription and desertion. Here, Hobbes implies that subjects' desertion in battle is cowardly but not unjust in some cases, and one of the stronger implications of the few paragraphs surrounding his brief discussion of desertion is that the obligations to serve the sovereign last only as long as the sovereign can guarantee its purpose, presumably the preservation of the lives and security of subjects. The question of how subjects in battle know that the sovereign fails on this front is open, suggesting that subjects' judgment still holds the authority to decide this critical question. For a philosophical argument for the Hobbesian subject's right to rebel, see Sreedhar, *Hobbes on Resistance*.

Chapter Three: The Risks of Political Authority

1. Baier, *Moral Prejudices*, 196. See also Luhmann, "Familiarity, Confidence, Trust." John Dunn, the preeminent interpreter of Locke on trust, phrases a similar idea differently: "Trust in the relation between ruled and ruler is not a supine psychic compulsion on the part of the former. Rather, it is an eminently realistic assessment of the irreversibility of a political division of labour and a sharp reminder, from the former to the latter, of the sole conditions that can make that division humanly benign." Dunn, "Trust and Political Agency," 87; and "'Trust' in the Politics of John Locke," 51.

2. The best work on the vulnerabilities and risks that characterize all trusting relationships remains Annette Baier's "Trust and Antitrust" and "Trust and its Vulnerabilities" in *Moral Prejudices*. The interpretive argument I make in this chapter and my overall claim in this book—that a study of risk helps us understand the meaning of trust

more clearly—depend on the ideas Baier advances in these pieces about the mutual constitution of trust and risk. Thanks to Karen Frost-Arnold for directing me to this work.

3. See Tarcov, "Locke's 'Second Treatise.'"

4. Locke's attention to uncertainty and the persistence of the contingent is well documented by scholars of prerogative, who establish that his "theory of prerogative is predicated on the assumption that the extraordinary is an ordinary part of politics." Fatovic, "Constitutionalism and Contingency," 282.

5. I cite Locke's work in the chapter's main text using the following abbreviations:

> *An Essay Concerning Human Understanding* is cited as *HU*, followed by book, chapter, and paragraph numbers.
> *Second Treatise of Government* is cited as *ST*, followed by paragraph number.
> *Further Considerations Concerning Raising the Value of Money* is cited as *FCM*, followed by the page number in the Kelly volumes.
> *Some Considerations on Lower Interest and Raising the Value of Money* is cited as *SCM*, followed by the page number in the Kelly volumes.

6. In all discussions of uncertainty and politics in the *Second Treatise*, Locke points to the "humane frailty" of those who rule, particularly princes.

7. See Corbett, "The Extraconstitutionality of Lockean Prerogative," 435.

8. Though this chapter focuses primarily on the legal analogy of trust that runs through the *Second Treatise*, the practice of trust is obviously embodied in the original compact as well, and in the more transient agreements that humans make in nature.

9. Pitkin, *The Concept of Representation*, 127–31.

10. See especially Gough, "Trusteeship." Gough's argument is a classic and offers convincing evidence that trust was a robust political metaphor in Locke's time, and that Locke would have known this and used it intentionally.

11. Laslett, "Introduction," 114–15.

12. Dunn, "'Trust' in the Politics of John Locke," 51. With respect to these latter claims about responsibility and psychological burdens, I am in agreement with Dunn, but I obviously disagree with the claim that the

metaphor does not do too much work for Locke otherwise. Joshua Dienstag persuasively argues against both Laslett and Dunn that we must pursue the metaphor to its endgame, in which beneficiaries are allowed to reclaim what is rightly theirs when trustees mishandle it. Dienstag, *Dancing in Chains*, 72.

13. Dunn's rich work on the concept of trust in Locke's thought alternately analyzes trust as a legal arrangement, as a strategic social and political practice that runs horizontally and vertically, and as a sentiment or passion akin to faith. Lockean trust is clearly multidimensional, and while I do not give equal time to each facet, all three dimensions appear in the *Second Treatise* and in the rest of Locke's corpus. The breakdown of any or all of them signals trouble for the stability of a political society. See especially Dunn, " 'Trust' in the Politics of John Locke" and "Trust and Political Agency."

14. A further complication is that Locke also links federative power—the power to conduct international relations—to the executive office by noting that federative and executive power are often held together in practice even though they are theoretically distinct. The executive can thus hold domestic and international power, as well as prerogative, and is meant to exercise all three in the common interest or common good. Add to this the elasticity of the "common good," the only entity trustees are meant to guard, and we must recognize that Locke leaves an unnerving degree of discretionary judgment and outsized power to the executive in practice. This arrangement may also contribute to the worry of many Locke scholars over prerogative as a strange and potentially destructive feature of Locke's thought. See Wolin, "Democracy and the Welfare State," 138.

15. Fatovic, "Constitutionalism and Contingency," 296.

16. See, for example, *ST*, 138 and 153.

17. For other examples of Locke's definitions of prerogative, see *ST*, 160, 164, 166, and 210.

18. Corbett, "The Extraconstitutionality of Lockean Prerogative," 430.

19. See also Corbett, "The Extraconstitutionality of Lockean Prerogative," 443.

20. Kleinerman, "Can the Prince Really Be Tamed?" 210.

21. See, for example, Corbett, "The Extraconstitutionality of Lockean Prerogative"; Fatovic, "Constitutionalism and Contingency"; and Kleinerman, "Can the Prince Really Be Tamed?"

22. Benjamin Kleinerman argues that Locke's insistence that obvious cases of tyranny are the norm reveals the inability of members of

the public to reflect in a sophisticated manner, beyond whether they personally benefit or suffer, on whether their political forms are in peril. Kleinerman, "Can the Prince Really Be Tamed?" 215. Leonard Feldman persuasively argues that this claim is complicated by Locke's own parallel examples of the proper exercise of prerogative and the undesirable exercise of tyranny, which resemble each other closely enough to require the careful exercise of judgment on the part of affected subjects. See Feldman, "Judging Necessity," 559–60.

23. The reference to "visibility" here is telling. To call something "visible" is, for Locke, to stress how powerfully evident it is. Locke notes in the *Essay* that sight is "the most instructive of our senses" (*HU,* 2.23.12). For a discussion of Locke's reliance on sight metaphors for indicating certainty, see Dawson, *Locke, Language, and Early-Modern Philosophy,* 246–47.

24. To apply the frequent risk rubric of "how likely? how bad?" to Locke's fire example, once we burn ourselves, we can know with pretty strong certitude how likely fire is to burn us if we touch it again, and we also know how badly it will hurt the next time.

25. As Douglas Casson writes, Locke's confidence that "the people can be made to see the clear signs of tyranny and distinguish them from the ordinary defects of government . . . rests on his belief that the judgment of the people is based on the hard currency of natural signs." Casson, *Liberating Judgment,* 249.

26. See Feldman "Judging Necessity," 562–63; and McClure, *Judging Rights,* 223–24.

27. Casson notes, by point of contrast with Hobbes, "Locke's insistence that the people exist as an independent and incorporated entity with the power to judge and not simply as a disorganized multitude of private judgments is central to his understanding of the regenerative possibilities of revolution." Locke, unlike Hobbes, "is convinced that his readers can and will exercise their judgment *as a people* with sober restraint and careful deliberation. His defense of the right of revolution rests on his assumption that the people will be able to form reasonable judgments about their condition." Casson, *Liberating Judgment,* 249; emphasis added. This may be an instance of Locke "bravely treading the path between hope and experience," in Hannah Dawson's words, given that it is likely to be very difficult for a multitude of individuals to communicate and form this kind of judgment. Dawson, *Locke, Language, and Early-Modern Philosophy,* 304.

28. Just who belongs in this deliberating, judging collective is something of a vexed problem in the Locke scholarship, but I lean toward the interpretation that Locke means his work on judgment, probability, and politics to encompass a wide public of "active" readers—the kinds of men for whom Hume also writes his essays. See also Casson, *Liberating Judgment*; Waldron, *God, Locke, and Equality*, ch. 5; and Wood, *The Politics of Locke's Philosophy*.

29. See Corbett, "The Extraconstitutionality of Lockean Prerogative," 447; and Feldman, *"Judging Necessity,"* 506.

30. The choice of "perhaps . . . not 12 *d.*" is significant because a shilling was the point at which larceny became punishable by death in English law, whereas a lesser amount provoked other corporal punishments such as whippings. See Coke, *The Third Part of the Institutes of the Laws of England*, 107.

31. This bears an interesting parallel with a moment in the introduction to the *Essay*, in which Locke points out that the inability to know everything should not stand in the way of man's pursuit of what he *can* understand. Here he writes, "'Tis of great use to the Sailor to know the lengths of his Line, though he cannot with it fathom all the depths of the Ocean. 'Tis well he knows, that it is long enough to reach the bottom, at such Places as are necessary to direct his Voyage, and caution him against running upon Shoals, that may ruin him" (*HU*, 1.5.28–31). As in the ship-to-Algiers metaphor, Locke here suggests that people must reason as far as they can to acquire the knowledge required for their own security and well-being.

32. In the *Essay*, Locke details how probable belief is acquired through the collection of observations, experiential knowledge, and the personal testimony of others (*HU*, 4.15.4–5).

33. Locke, *Of the Conduct of the Understanding*, 180–81. This raises a question about the role of elites in Locke's politics, a question taken up by scholars of prerogative and revolution. Tarcov and Kleinerman argue for versions of elite cueing, whereas other Locke interpreters, like Casson and Feldman, argue that the burdens of all kinds of judgments belong with a range of political actors. See Tarcov "Locke's 'Second Treatise,'" 214; Kleinerman, "Can the Prince Really Be Tamed?"; Casson, *Liberating Judgment*; and Feldman, "Judging Necessity." I lean heavily toward the latter interpretation, including all men of action rather than a narrow class of political elites, although there is evidence for the former. I would insist, however, that Locke excludes here those who are typically marginalized in

seventeenth-century political communities: women, slaves, manual laborers, the nonworking poor, the disabled, and children.

34. Dienstag, *Dancing in Chains*, 71.

35. As the *Second Treatise*'s chapters on usurpation and conquest show, however, Locke suggests that communities ought to have persistent concerns about external states and armies, too.

36. For example, in Locke's writings on the problem of interest, he argues that the rate of interest should not be raised or lowered by decree of law, but should be determined by the vicissitudes of a commercial market. In Locke's papers from the 1690s, he argues for this position by framing the efforts to legally lower the rate of interest as disproportionately risky, since it seemed likely to engender financial losses without compensating or exceeding profits (*SCM*, 220, 242, 276, 297). There is an interesting shift between early drafts and final drafts of *Some Considerations on Lower Interest and Raising the Value of Money*, pertaining to the language Locke uses. In the early drafts, there is no mention of "risk" ("risque," for Locke). He spent nearly four decades working out his opposition to arguments for the lowering of interest, and some time before the final 1691 draft, he uses "risque" to describe an outsized loss that might come from tampering with the interest rate to lower it, either in place of the words he used in prior drafts, like "venture," or as a new way of framing his disagreement with advocates of fixing the rate by law. These comparisons were drawn from materials in Locke ms. d. 2, John Locke Manuscripts, Lovelace Collection, Bodleian Library, Oxford University, containing early drafts with handwritten revisions.

37. On the coinage controversy, see Peter Kelly's introduction to the collected economic writings of Locke. Kelly, "General Introduction," 1–151. Casson draws an intriguing parallel between Locke's worry about coinage and his worry about language, arguing that both were symptoms of a broad epistemological crisis. Casson, *Liberating Judgment*, 1–11. Dawson also emphasizes the coinage crisis as a moment of profound crisis for public trust, near the end of her book on the instability of language and the problems this creates for political trust. Dawson, *Locke, Language, and Early-Modern Philosophy*, 288. On the connection between money and epistemology in the *Second Treatise*, see also Ince, "Enclosing in God's Name, Accumulating for Mankind."

38. Carl Wennerlind connects the Great Recoinage to the Financial Revolution, and argues that the monetary crisis was in fact a credit crisis. To support this view, he explores how the death penalty was used to

deter coin debasement, in hopes that it would restore public faith in the coin, its value, and existing networks of trust, credit, and exchange. Wennerlind, *Casualties of Credit.*

39. Casson, *Liberating Judgment*, 4. Muldrew emphasizes that it is nearly impossible to parse social exchange and economic change in this period, so a breakdown in trust and credit in the world of exchange also rends social and political trust to shreds. Muldrew, *The Economy of Obligation*, ch. 7.

40. Smith puts this very well in a discussion of coin debasement in his lectures on jurisprudence, given roughly seventy years after Locke was involved in the recoinage:

> The inconveniences of such practices are very great. The debasement of the coin hinders commerce or at least greatly embarrasses it. A new calculation must be made, how much of the new coin must be given for so much of the old. People are disposed to keep their goods from the market, as they know not what they will get for them. Thus a stagnation of commerce is occasioned. Besides, the debasing of the coin *takes away the public faith.* Nobody will lend any sum to the government, or bargain with it, as he may perhaps be paid with one half of it. (*Lectures on Jurisprudence*, 502; emphasis added)

41. Locke was also extremely worried about how the currency crisis had forced a turn to paper money, which relied wholly on trust and credit for its values—a dangerous prospect in a world with thieves and counterfeiters successfully damaging coin (*FCM*, 450–51).

42. Locke, for all his innovations regarding flux and intersubjectivity in the political realm, had a common but rigid understanding of wealth as fixed in the amount of hard currency—in this case, silver—that a person or a state possessed.

43. Kelly, "General Introduction," 90–91; Casson, *Liberating Judgment*, 253.

Chapter Four: Hume's Fine Balance

1. I cite Hume's work in the text with the following abbreviations:

> *An Enquiry Concerning Human Understanding* is cited as *EHU*, followed by chapter and section numbers.
> *Essays Moral, Political and Literary* is cited as *EMPL.*

The History of England is cited as *HE*, followed by volume number.
A Treatise of Human Nature is cited as *T*, followed by book, part, section, and paragraph numbers.

All are cited by page number from the particular editions listed in the reference list.

2. See *An Enquiry Concerning Human Understanding*, where Hume notes that "experimental inference and reasoning concerning the actions of others enters so much into human life that no man, while awake, is ever a moment without employing it" (*EHU*, 8.17, 80).

3. As Mary Poovey puts it, "One facet of Hume's skepticism follow[s] his recognition that the map of human motivation produced by the moral philosopher would inevitably be colored by his own attitude toward himself." Poovey, *A History of the Modern Fact*, 199.

4. Donald Livingston argues that Hume's variety of

> philosophical reflection . . . must work . . . both within and without the world of common life. It works within insofar as the authority of common life as a whole is internal to philosophical thinking. It works without insofar as the philosopher can frame abstract ideals and principles which can be used to correct any particular belief or maxim of common life in the light of other beliefs and maxims considered at the time to be unproblematic. (Livingston, *Hume's Philosophy of Common Life*, 30)

5. The definition of "risk" offered by David Garland in his essay "The Rise of Risk" captures this: "Risk begins where certain knowledge ends. Claims about risk are, literally, uncertain knowledge claims— impressionistic guesses, informed estimates, and probabilistic predictions about a future that cannot fully be known." Garland, "The Rise of Risk," 50–51.

6. Perhaps this point is best stated by John Locke in his *Essay Concerning Human Understanding*, a text Hume certainly contends with in his *Treatise*, when Locke notes that "even the highest probability amounts not to certainty, without which there can be no *true* knowledge" (*HU*, 4.3.14). Hume admits this, but his point is that we need to use what we have, and what we have is probability.

7. Hacking points out that Hume sticks fairly closely here to established ideas of knowledge (as the product of demonstration) and probability. Where Hume does something a bit different is to argue that some probabilities deserve the status of proof, in effect establishing that

probabilistic knowledge does not have to be unstable. He also moves the study of causation squarely into the realm of probability. See Hacking, *The Emergence of Probability*, 180–81.

8. Gower, "Hume on Probability."

9. Since Hume will assert that both are quantifiable in similar ways, perhaps he has cause to think it is hard to tell the difference.

10. Cf. *T*, 1.3.11.6, 87: "Where nothing limits the chances, every notion, that the most extravagant fancy can form, is upon a footing of equality; nor can there be any circumstances to give one the advantage above the other."

11. Hume's calculation of the strength of belief likely seems odd. As he explains, we stand a four-in-six chance of turning up an X and a two-in-six chance of turning up a Y when we throw the die. Each face earns 1/6 of our belief in its likelihood of landing face up; thus X gets 4/6 of our belief, and Y gets an inferior 2/6 of our belief. Where Hume surprises us is with the claim that because the events (throwing X or throwing Y) are opposed and mutually exclusive, the belief in the inferior outcome cancels out a portion of our impulse to expect the superior outcome. The way he calculates it, we must subtract our impulse to expect a Y from our impulse to expect an X (4 − 2), thus leaving ourselves with only a two-times stronger probable belief that we will see an X and, curiously, no belief that we will see a Y when we toss the die (*T*, 1.3.12, 89). Gower suggests that Hume runs together mathematical probability and jurisprudential approaches to probability and degrees of certainty. Gower, "Hume on Probability," 7–9.

12. Gower, "Hume on Probability," 10.

13. See also *T*, 1.3.12.3, 90.

14. As Lorraine Daston explains, though this habit "may not be strictly rational . . . it is exact." Daston, Classical *Probability in the Enlightenment*, 201.

15. For the purposes of understanding Hume's point of view on risk, I mostly emphasize the *Treatise*'s consideration of how uncertainty induces fear in us. But I would emphasize again that an acceptance of uncertainty is also the basis of Hume's commitment to his mitigated variety of skepticism, which undermines dogmatism. Read in this way, his works suggest that while living with uncertainty might be painful, it also does us good (*EHU*, 12.24, 140–41). Thanks to Dennis Rasmussen for this point.

16. Think, Hume suggests, of a nervous bride on her wedding night (*T*, 2.3.9.29, 286).

17. David Wootton argues that Hume expends a fair bit of energy trying to exclude contingency from his philosophy, precisely because he is so sensitive to how it wears on human beings. He suggests that Hume's own uneasiness about uncertainty drives him to resist any indication that accidents play a deciding role in human affairs. See Wootton, "From Fortune to Feedback," 37–38. This seems incorrect to me; Hume thinks that uncertainty breeds a certain healthy skepticism in us that is perhaps worth the cost of the affective burden it puts on us, but he still acknowledges its debilitating effects.

18. As Daston explains in her interpretation of Hume on risk and uncertainty, "Fear has the upper hand, even in situations which on the strength of Hume's own analysis should instead produce hope. This is the frame of mind that magnifies misfortunes, and shuns risk." Daston, *Classical Probability in the Enlightenment*, 186. Hume's friend Adam Smith seems to hold this view as well, as we find in a rather humorous digression on beer tax in the *Lectures on Jurisprudence*: "Man is an anxious animal and must have his care swept off by something that can exhilarate the spirits," he writes with some sympathy. Smith, *Lectures on Jurisprudence*, 497.

19. Daston argues that the orientation toward risk that Hume theorizes in his work on probability and the future only deepens in the decades following his work, and she notes it as a curious product of two emergent conditions in the late eighteenth and early nineteenth centuries. First, life was becoming more stable and secure, such that many people were spared daily confrontation with preventable risks (e.g., disease, war, starvation). This daily reprieve left them more time and energy to imagine and contemplate an unknown future. If Hume is right, this imaginative process might be more conducive to fear or terror than the experience of confronting daunting troubles head on. Second, for many of these people, their stability and insulation from direct confrontation with avoidable harms depended on very recent gains from trade and professional labor. Taken together, these two conditions produced a commercial class of people who, when contemplating the future, vividly anticipated both probable and improbable risks with extreme trepidation.

Daston's analysis also contrasts gambling and insurance practices as two sides of risk in the Enlightenment. As expected, the long tradition of gambling encourages the view that taking risks is, in effect, exploiting opportunities for gain and profit. The hallmark passion of the gambler is, on this read, hope for a big but improbable win.

For the burgeoning insurance industry, the perspective is totally opposite. Daston interestingly traces the ways in which insurance practitioners adopted statistical methods rather late, because the insurance business was deeply rooted in exploiting anxiety about *all* risk, and hence insurers were uninterested in parsing probable from improbable risks by crunching the numbers. She notes that, by the nineteenth century, the insurance perspective had won out—even gamblers were starting to preach prudence and trepidation. She links this insurance model closely to Hume's point of view on probability and affect. See Daston, Classical *Probability in the Enlightenment*, 185–87.

20. Norton, "An Introduction to Hume's Thought," 5.
21. Most uses of the word "risk" in Hume's corpus appear in discussions of publishing found in his correspondence with friends and conversation partners, showing that he viewed risk as an aspect of his own transactions and exchanges.
22. On Hume's practice of essay writing, see especially Sitter, *Literary Loneliness in Mid-Eighteenth-Century England*, ch. 1; and Christensen, *Practicing Enlightenment*, chs. 3 and 5. On the possibilities of the essay form as a genre of political theory, see Panagia, "The Force of Political Argument."
23. The historian seems to be especially good at striking this balance. Consider the following, from Hume's essay "On the Study of History":

> When a man of business enters into life and action, he is more apt to consider the characters of men, as they have relation to his interest, than as they stand in themselves; and has his judgment warped on every occasion by the violence of his passion. When a philosopher contemplates characters and manners in his closet, the general abstract view of the objects leaves the mind so cold and unmoved, that the sentiments of nature have no room to play, and he scarce feels the difference between vice and virtue. History keeps in a just medium betwixt these extremes, and places the objects in their true point of view. (*EMPL*, 568)

This ability to find a "true point of view" of course depends on the presumed balance of the historian, who cares enough about the characters and events to plot a lively narrative, but not so much that this narrative is corrupted by inappropriate passions. In any case, Hume argues that the historian, who deals in experience over the long term, manages to avoid the pitfalls of "mere philosophy" and "mere ignorance."

24. Although I have largely focused on Hume's depiction of human beings as quite anxious people, his commitment to intellectual exchange, mediated by the essay form, reflects another side of Hume's views on what human beings are like—curious and conversational. As Emma Rothschild explains, "The discursive, inquisitive men and women who are at the heart of [Hume's] description of human nature are continuously recounting and receiving information; they are also continuously looking for new sources of intelligence and trying to decide whether pieces of information are true." Rothschild, "The Atlantic Worlds of David Hume," 420.

25. On the epistemological purposes of Hume's essays, I have found especially helpful Mary Poovey's *A History of the Modern Fact*, which dedicates a section of its chapter on experimental moral philosophy to Hume's skepticism and turn to the essay form. See also Wulf, "The Skeptical Life in Hume's Political Thought." Wulf argues that Hume's skepticism is mitigated *and* sustained by a life dedicated to doing philosophy in the context of social, political, and economic transactions.

26. Jerome Christensen points to Hume's experience in the world of commerce as the resource he draws on to run together knowledge production and commercial practice. See Christensen, *Practicing Enlightenment*, 151–52.

27. Emphasis added. James Conniff argues that Hume is "disingenuous" in "That Politics May Be Reduced to a Science," claiming that Hume's real purpose is to undercut the certain claims about politics offered by English republicans like James Harrington by generating counterclaims of his own, thus opening the door for a moderate politics rooted in compromise. See Conniff, "Hume's Political Methodology," 80, 106.

28. See Sabl, "When Bad Things Happen from Good People (and Vice-Versa)," 78.

29. Poovey interprets this rather peculiar juxtaposition as an indication that Hume is leaving open the question of political knowledge for his readers to consider and inviting them to join him in argument. Poovey, *A History of the Modern Fact*, 209.

30. Admittedly, "mercantilism" is a rather problematic shorthand long used by scholars of political economy, usually to describe a set of arguments in circulation in the seventeenth and eighteenth centuries. It generally assumes that before free trade took hold as an ideology,

political economists were in agreement about economic goals for the state, and that many of the goals were underpinned by the belief that wealth was finite. In recent years, scholars have usefully complicated this story about what mercantilism was, instead describing it as a varied set of arguments among political economists about labor, trade, statecraft, and improvement. To offer only two examples, see Stern and Wennerlind, *Mercantilism Reimagined,* which offers a collection of revisionist essays on different aspects of mercantile thought; and Pincus, "Rethinking Mercantilism."

31. Here, Hume begins a critique that will shape Smith's analysis of joint-stock companies in *The Wealth of Nations,* which, I argue, turns on a particular understanding of how these companies manage risk poorly.

32. This assumption that actors require a push to boldness, a call to the bolder passions, in order to pursue their interests is a bit of an inversion of Albert Hirschman's thesis in *The Passions and the Interests.*

33. On this point, see Christensen, *Practicing Enlightenment,* 148–50.

34. Part of this argument, and a major theme of all Hume's economic writings, is the claim that "the real riches of a country were in her people, skills and materials," rather than her stock of hard currency. Hont, *Jealousy of Trade,* 279.

35. Grüne-Yanoff and McClennen, "Hume's Framework for a Natural History of the Passions," 89.

36. This example will also figure in the next chapter, presented there as the root of Smith's arguments against the balance of trade doctrine.

37. Although Hume argues that all parties (in this case, all states) will benefit from a system of free trade, he is not arguing that the outcomes will be uniform or equal among trading nations. The commercial prosperity of each trading nation will depend on other factors as well, like institutions, manners, and climates; the absolute outcomes will vary from place to place. His point is simply that all states can benefit from an open system, a point underscored by many interpreters of Hume's theories of money and international trade. See Cheney, "Constitution and Economy in David Hume's Enlightenment," 228–29; Hont, *Jealousy of Trade,* 270–72; and Hont, "The 'Rich Country–Poor Country' Debate Revisited," 213–14.

Chapter Five: Adventurous Spirits and Clamoring Sophists

1. For Smith, however, risk is not a problem confined to politics and economy. He writes about risk more generally as simply a fact of life.

For example, in his *Lectures on Jurisprudence*, he uses the word "risk" (sometimes spelled "risque") repeatedly to describe all types of dangers, harms, and hazards. As this chapter will show, his attention to economic risk is more precise and includes treatment of its profit potential, too.

2. Smith's account also has antiheroic dimensions. Emma Rothschild and Amartya Sen note that traders and their partners in manufacture are "the heroes . . . of the epic of increasing opulence which was at the heart of Smith's economic thought" and "at the same time its 'sneaking' hypocrites." Rothschild and Sen, "Adam Smith's Economics," 328.

3. I cite Smith's work in the text using the following abbreviations:

    > *An Inquiry into the Nature and Causes of the Wealth of Nations* is cited as *WN*, followed by book, chapter, and section numbers. Page numbers are cited from the edition listed in the reference list.
    >
    > *Lectures on Jurisprudence* is cited as *LJ*, followed by the page number from the edition listed in the reference list.
    >
    > *The Theory of Moral Sentiments* is cited as *TMS*, followed by part, chapter, and section numbers. Page numbers are cited from the edition listed in the reference list.

4. See also Pocock, *The Machiavellian Moment,* for an account of earlier British debates on the relationship between economic habits, reputation, and credit, which certainly prefigure and inform Smith's commentary.

5. Smith's evaluation of political economy distinguishes sharply between "*individual* pursuit of self-interest under competitive conditions, when all the rules of fair play and strict justice are being observed, and *collective* pursuit of self-interest through combination, monopoly and extra-parliamentary pressure-group activity." Winch, *Riches and Poverty,* 108.

6. For all these reasons, Joseph Cropsey stresses that "a point on which Smith is most emphatic is that the mercantile class must not rule." Cropsey, *Polity and Economy,* 78.

7. Smith does acknowledge that joint-stock companies may have temporary uses when it comes to managing risk and encouraging desirable risk taking, in much the same way temporary monopolies might protect novel inventions. This harkens back to the kinds of argu-

ments Hume makes about encouraging risk taking, which can appear too daunting in many contexts. Smith writes:

> *When* a *company* of *merchants undertake,* at *their own risk and expence,* to *establish* a *new trade* with some remote *and* barbarous nation, it may not be unreasonable to incorporate them into a joint stock *company, and* to grant them, in case of *their* success, a monopoly of the *trade* for a certain number of years. It is the easiest *and* most natural way in which the state can recompense them for hazarding a dangerous *and* expensive experiment, of which the publick is afterwards to reap the benefit. A temporary monopoly of this kind may be vindicated upon the same principles upon which a like monopoly of a *new* machine is granted to its inventor, *and* that of a *new* book to its author. (*WN*, 5.1e.9)

His indictment of joint-stock companies has more to do with their persistence and long-term effects and practices after their initial usefulness has expired.

8. For an argument that depicts joint-stock companies *as* sovereigns, with a special focus on the East India Company, see Stern, *The Company State.*

9. Muthu, "Adam Smith's Critique of International Trading Companies," 187. Muthu attends carefully to how these companies become de facto sovereigns in the far reaches of British empire, and he analyzes Smith's strong criticism of their governing practices.

10. On Smith's place in the tradition of thought on corruption, see Hill, "Adam Smith on the Theme of Corruption."

11. As Istvan Hont puts it, "For Smith, the commercial nation was first and foremost a community of consumers. The interest of merchants and manufacturers was secondary. *Salus populi,* true reason of state, entailed that the interest of consumers trump the interest of producers." Hont, *Jealousy of Trade,* 55.

12. Later, Smith points out that monopolies have strengthened the order of merchants so greatly that they are well positioned to intimidate legislators, and that they in fact do (*WN,* 4.2.43, 471).

13. Hont, *Jealousy of Trade,* 54.

14. Ibid., 54–55.

15. Bentham, *A Defense of Usury,* 13.3–4. Emphasis added.

16. Ibid., 13.6.

17. Ibid., 30.28.

18. As Charles Griswold notes, Smith distinguishes among different types of prudence in his work. This chapter is concerned with what Griswold calls "ordinary prudence," the virtue of economic actors that drives them to approach the maintenance and improvement of fortune with skill and caution. Griswold, *Adam Smith and the Virtues of Enlightenment*, 203. On prudence as the primary economic virtue in Smith's work, see also Hanley, *Adam Smith and the Character of Virtue*, 100–31.

19. For Smith, "Prudence should thus both guide men to secure their own fortunes in the long term and also promote economic growth; merchants fail on the first count, and *Wealth of Nations* analyzes the lost possibilities for economic growth in light of their failures." Mehta, "Self-Interest and Other Interests," 259–62. See also Hanley, *Adam Smith and the Character of Virtue*, 115.

20. As Charles Griswold rightly insists, the prudent person is "not a mere monad in a society of strangers, intent just on improving his or her material lot, and a society of prudent persons is not a formula for social anomie. The prudent person has moral ties to others, including those of benevolence and justice, and exhibits other virtues as well." Griswold, *Adam Smith and the Virtues of Enlightenment*, 206.

21. Hont, *Jealousy of Trade*, 360–61.

Chapter Six: An Age of Risk, a Liberalism of Anxiety

1. Foucault, *The Birth of Biopolitics*, 66–67.

2. Freedgood analyzes these kinds of phenomena in *Victorian Writing about Risk*, arguing that Victorian Britain found consolation and temporary relief from a culture of danger, contingency, and risk in hygiene pamphlets, travel and adventure literature, and other ephemeral texts in circulation.

3. For a history of fear and its relation to modern politics, see Robin, *Fear*, 27–160.

4. In a way, this suggestion runs in parallel to the analysis we find in Mary Douglas's *Risk and Blame*. She notes that even as our tools for calculating risks and measuring probable outcomes have become more refined and precise, our risk discourse has failed to match their precision. As she argues, when we use the word "risk" in everyday discourse, especially political discourse, we rarely refer to a probabilistic prediction of a likely future outcome. Rather, we use the word "risk"

to signal a perceived danger, which leads Douglas to suggest that by calling something a risk and not simply a danger, we try to draw on the scientific authority linked to probability studies and the calculation of risk to support our sense that we are facing something bad. That is, "risk" bears a certain authority and urgency that mere "danger" does not. For Douglas, this lack of clarity when it comes to our terms is troubling and worth consideration, just as we might give more thought to the persistent impulse to run together risk and uncertainty. See Douglas, *Risk and Blame*, especially chapter 1.

REFERENCES

Abizadeh, Arash. 2013. "The Representation of Hobbesian Sovereignty: Leviathan as Mythology." In *Hobbes Today: Insights for the 21st Century.* Ed. S. A. Lloyd. New York: Cambridge University Press, 113–52.

Adams, John. 1995. *Risk.* London: UCL Press.

Ashcraft, Richard. 1978. "Ideology and Class in Hobbes' Political Theory." *Political Theory* 6 (2): 27–62.

Baier, Annette. 1995. *Moral Prejudices: Essays on Ethics.* Cambridge, MA: Harvard University Press.

Beck, Ulrich. 1992. *Risk Society: Towards a New Modernity.* Trans. Mark Ritter. London: Sage Publications.

———. 1999. *World Risk Society.* Cambridge: Polity Press.

Bentham, Jeremy. 1787. *A Defence of Usury.* Library of Economics and Liberty. Accessed December 1, 2011. http://www.econlib.org/library /Bentham/bnthUs3.html.

Bernstein, Peter. 1998. *Against the Gods: The Remarkable Story of Risk.* New York: Wiley.

Borot, Luc. 1996. "History in Hobbes' Thought." In *The Cambridge Companion to Hobbes.* Ed. Tom Sorrell. Cambridge: Cambridge University Press, 305–28.

Casson, Douglas John. 2011. *Liberating Judgment: Fanatics, Skeptics, and John Locke's Politics of Probability.* Princeton, NJ: Princeton University Press.

Cheney, Paul. 2009. "Constitution and Economy in David Hume's Enlightenment." In *David Hume's Political Economy.* Ed. Carl Wennerlind and Margaret Schabas. London: Routledge, 223–42.

Christensen, Jerome. 1987. *Practicing Enlightenment: Hume and the Formation of a Literary Career.* Madison: University of Wisconsin Press.

Coke, Edward. 1809. *The Third Part of the Institutes of the Laws of England: Concerning High Treason and Other Pleas of the Crown and Criminal Causes.* London: W. Clarke and Sons.

Collins, Jeffrey R. 2005. *The Allegiance of Thomas Hobbes.* Oxford: Oxford University Press.

Conniff, James. 1976. "Hume's Political Methodology: A Reconsideration of 'That Politics May Be Reduced to a Science.'" *Review of Politics* 38 (1): 88–108.

Corbett, Ross. 2006. "The Extraconstitutionality of Lockean Prerogative." *Review of Politics* 68: 428–48.

Cropsey, Joseph. 2001. *Polity and Economy, With Further Thoughts on the Principles of Adam Smith.* South Bend, IN: St. Augustine's Press.

Daston, Lorraine. 1995. *Classical Probability in the Enlightenment.* Princeton, NJ: Princeton University Press.

Dawson, Hannah. 2007. *Locke, Language, and Early-Modern Philosophy.* Cambridge: Cambridge University Press.

Dean, Mitchell. 1999. *Governmentality: Power and Rule in Modern Society.* London: Sage Publications.

Dienstag, Joshua Foa. 1997. *Dancing in Chains: Narrative and Memory in Political Theory.* Stanford, CA: Stanford University Press.

Douglas, Mary. 1994. *Risk and Blame: Essays in Cultural Theory.* London: Routledge.

Drucker, Fred. 1983. *The Practice of Management.* New York: Harper Business.

Dunn, John. 1985. "'Trust' in the Politics of John Locke." In *Rethinking Modern Political Theory: Essays, 1979–83.* Cambridge: Cambridge University Press, 34–54.

———. 1990. "Trust and Political Agency." In *Trust: Making and Breaking Cooperative Relations.* Ed. Diego Gambetta. London: Blackwell, 73–93.

Ewald, François. "Two Infinities of Risk." In *The Politics of Everyday Fear.* Ed. Brian Massumi. Minneapolis: University of Minnesota Press, 221–28.

Fatovic, Clement. 2004. "Constitutionalism and Contingency: Locke's Theory of Prerogative." *History of Political Thought* 25 (2): 276–97.

Feldman, Leonard C. 2008. "Judging Necessity." *Political Theory* 26 (4): 550–77.

Foucault, Michel. 1991. "Governmentality." In *The Foucault Effect: Studies in Governmentality with Two Lectures by and an Interview with Michel Foucault.* Ed. Colin Gordon, Graham Burchell, and Peter Miller. Chicago, IL: University of Chicago Press, 87–104.

———. 2009. *Security, Territory, Population: Lectures at the Collège de France, 1977–1978.* New York: Picador.

———. 2010. *The Birth of Biopolitics: Lectures at the Collège de France, 1978–1979.* New York: Picador.

Franklin, Jane. 2006. "Politics and Risk." In *Beyond the Risk Society: Critical Reflections on Risk and Human Security*. Ed. Gabe Mythen and Sandra Walklate. New York: Open University Press, 149–68.

Freedgood, Elaine. 2006. *Victorian Writing About Risk: Imagining a Safe England in a Dangerous World*. Cambridge: Cambridge University Press.

Garland, David. 2003. "The Rise of Risk." In *Risk and Morality*. Ed. Aaron Doyle and Richard V. Ericson. Toronto: University of Toronto Press, 48–86.

Garrett, Don. 2002. "Hume on Testimony Concerning Miracles." In *Reading Hume on Human Understanding*. Ed. Peter Millican. Oxford: Oxford University Press, 301–34.

Gauthier, David. 1968. *The Logic of Leviathan*. Oxford: Oxford University Press.

Giddens, Anthony. 1991. *Modernity and Self-Identity: Self and Society in the Late Modern Age*. Stanford, CA: Stanford University Press.

Gigerenzer, Gerd, Zeno Swijtink, Theodore Porter, Lorraine Daston, John Beatty, and Lorenz Krüger, eds. 1990. *The Empire of Chance: How Probability Changed Science and Everyday Life*. Cambridge: Cambridge University Press.

Gordon, Colin, Graham Burchell, and Peter Miller, eds. *The Foucault Effect: Studies in Governmentality with Two Lectures by and an Interview with Michel Foucault*. Chicago, IL: University of Chicago Press.

Gough, J. W. 1956. "Trusteeship." In *John Locke's Political Philosophy: Eight Studies*. Oxford: Clarendon Press, 137–71.

Gower, Barry. 1991. "Hume on Probability." *British Journal for the Philosophy of Science* 42 (1): 1–19.

Griswold, Charles. 1999. *Adam Smith and the Virtues of Enlightenment*. Cambridge: Cambridge University Press.

Grüne-Yanoff, Till, and Edward McClennen. 2009. "Hume's Framework for a Natural History of the Passions." In *David Hume's Political Economy*. Ed. Carl Wennerlind and Margaret Schabas. London: Routledge, 86–104.

Hacking, Ian. 1984. *The Emergence of Probability: A Philosophical Study of Early Ideas about Probability, Induction and Statistical Inference*. Cambridge: Cambridge University Press.

———. 1990. *The Taming of Chance*. Cambridge: Cambridge University Press.

———. 2003. "Risk and Dirt." In *Risk and Morality*. Ed. Aaron Doyle and Richard V. Ericson. Toronto: University of Toronto Press, 22–47.

Hampton, Jean. 1986. *Hobbes and the Social Contract Tradition.* Cambridge: Cambridge University Press.

Hanley, Ryan. 2011. *Adam Smith and the Character of Virtue.* Cambridge: Cambridge University Press.

Hill, Lisa. 2006. "Adam Smith on the Theme of Corruption." *Review of Politics* 68: 636–62.

Hirschman, Albert O. 1997. *The Passions and the Interests: Political Arguments for Capitalism Before its Triumph.* Princeton, NJ: Princeton University Press.

Hobbes, Thomas. 1656. *Six Lessons to the Professors of the Mathematiques, one of Geometry, the other of Astronomy: In the Chaires set up by the Noble and Learned Sir Henry Savile, in the University of Oxford.* In *Elements of Philosophy, the First Section Concerning the Body. Written in Latine by Thomas Hobbes of Malmesbury and now Translated into English.* London: R. and W. Leybourne for Andrew Crocke at the Greene Dragon in Paul's Church-yard.

———. 1843. "Dedication." *The History of the Grecian War, Written By Thucydides.* In *The English Works of Thomas Hobbes of Malmsbury.* Vol. 8. Ed. Sir William Molesworth. London: Bohn, iii–vi.

———. 1843. "Of the Life and History of Thucydides." *The History of the Grecian War, Written By Thucydides.* In *The English Works of Thomas Hobbes of Malmsbury.* Vol. 8. Ed. Sir William Molesworth. London: Bohn, xiii–xxxii.

———. 1843. "To the Readers." *The History of the Grecian War, Written By Thucydides.* In *The English Works of Thomas Hobbes of Malmsbury.* Vol. 8. Ed. Sir William Molesworth. London: Bohn, vii–xi.

———. 1990. *Behemoth, or the Long Parliament.* Ed. Stephen Holmes. Chicago, IL: University of Chicago Press.

———. 1994. *De Corpore.* In *Human Nature and De Corpore Politico.* Ed. J.C.A. Gaskin. Oxford: Oxford University Press, 109–228.

———. 1994. *The Elements of Law.* In *Human Nature and De Corpore Politico.* Ed. J.C.A. Gaskin. Oxford: Oxford University Press, 21–108.

———. 1994. *Leviathan.* Translated by Edwin Curley. Indianapolis: Hackett Publishing.

———. 1998. *On the Citizen.* Ed. Richard Tuck and Michael Silverthorne. Cambridge: Cambridge University Press.

Hont, Istvan. 2005. *Jealousy of Trade: International Competition and the Nation-State in Historical Perspective.* Cambridge, MA: Harvard University Press.

———. 2009. "The 'Rich Country–Poor Country' Debate Revisited: The Irish Origins and French Reception of the Hume Paradox." In *David Hume's Political Economy.* Ed. Carl Wennerlind and Margaret Schabas. London: Routledge, 243–322.

Hume, David. 1983. *The History of England from the Invasion of Julius Caesar to the Revolution in 1688.* Ed. William B. Todd. Indianapolis, IN: Liberty Fund.

———. 1985. *Essays Moral, Political and Literary.* Indianapolis, IN: Liberty Fund.

———. 2000. *A Treatise of Human Nature.* Ed. David Fate Norton and Mary J. Norton. Oxford: Oxford University Press.

———. 2007. *An Enquiry Concerning Human Understanding and Other Writings.* Ed. Stephen Buckle. Cambridge: Cambridge University Press.

Ince, Onur Ulas. 2011. "Enclosing in God's Name, Accumulating for Mankind: Money, Morality, and Accumulation in John Locke's Theory of Property." *Review of Politics* 70 (1): 29–54.

Jesseph, Douglas. 1996. "Hobbes and the Method of Natural Science." In *The Cambridge Companion to Hobbes.* Ed. Tom Sorrell. Cambridge: Cambridge University Press, 86–107.

———. 2000. *Squaring the Circle: The War Between Hobbes and Wallis.* Chicago, IL: University of Chicago Press.

Kahn, Victoria. 2001. "Hobbes, Romance, and the Contract of Mimesis." *Political Theory* 29 (1): 4–29.

———. 2005. *Wayward Contracts: The Crisis of Political Obligation in England, 1640–1674.* Princeton, NJ: Princeton University Press.

Kelly, Peter. 1991. "General Introduction: Locke on Money." In *Locke on Money.* Vol. 1. Oxford: Clarendon Press, 1–151.

Kleinerman, Benjamin A. 2007. "Can the Prince Really Be Tamed? Executive Prerogative, Popular Apathy, and the Constitutional Frame in Locke's *Second Treatise.*" *American Political Science Review* 101 (2): 209–22.

Knight, Frank. 1964. *Risk, Uncertainty, and Profit.* New York: August M. Kelley.

Kraynak, Robert P. 1982. "Hobbes's *Behemoth* and the Argument for Absolutism." *American Political Science Review* 76 (4): 837–47.

Laslett, Peter. 1960. "Introduction." In *Two Treatises of Government.* Cambridge: Cambridge University Press, 3–120.

Leeuwen, Henry G. Van. 1963. *The Problem of Certainty in English Thought: 1630–1690.* The Hague: Martinus Nijhoff.

Levy, Jonathan. 2012. *Freaks of Fortune: The Emerging World of Capitalism and Risk in America.* Cambridge, MA: Harvard University Press.

Livingston, Donald W. 1984. *Hume's Philosophy of Common Life.* Chicago, IL: University of Chicago Press.

Locke, John., Manuscripts. Lovelace Collection. Bodleian Library, Oxford University.

———. 1978. *An Essay Concerning Human Understanding.* Ed. Peter Nidditch. Oxford: Clarendon Press.

———. 1988. *Second Treatise.* In *Two Treatises of Government.* Ed. Peter Laslett. Cambridge: Cambridge University Press, 265–428.

———. 1991. *Some Considerations of the Consequences of the Lowering of Interest, and Raising the Value of Money.* In *Locke on Money.* Vol 1. Oxford: Clarendon Press, 203–342.

———. 1991. *Further Considerations Concerning Raising the Value of Money.* In *Locke on Money.* Vol. 2. Oxford: Clarendon Press, 400–81.

———. 1996. *Some Thoughts Concerning Education; and, Of the Conduct of the Understanding.* Ed. Ruth W. Grant and Nathan Tarcov. Indianapolis: Hackett.

Luhmann, Niklas. 1990. "Familiarity, Confidence, Trust: Problems and Alternatives." In *Trust: Making and Breaking Cooperative Relations.* Ed. Diego Gambetta. London: Blackwell, 94–107.

———. 1993. *Risk: A Sociological Theory.* Trans. Rhodes Barrett. New York: Aldine.

Malcolm, Noel. 2002. *Aspects of Hobbes.* Oxford: Clarendon Press.

Mathiowetz, Dean. 2011. *Appeals to Interest: Language, Contestation, and the Shape of Political Agency.* University Park, PA: Penn State University Press.

Mehta, Pratap Bhanu. 2006. "Self-Interest and Other Interests." In *The Cambridge Companion to Adam Smith.* Ed. Knud Haakonsen. Cambridge: Cambridge University Press, 246–69.

Muldrew, Craig. 1998. *The Economy of Obligation: The Culture of Credit and Social Relations in Early Modern England.* London: Palgrave.

Muthu, Sankar. 2008. "Adam Smith's Critique of International Trading Companies: Theorizing 'Globalization' in the Age of Enlightenment." *Political Theory* 36 (2): 185–212.

McClure, Kirstie. 1996. *Judging Rights: Lockean Politics and the Limits of Consent.* Ithaca, NY: Cornell University Press.

Norton, David Fate. 1993. "An Introduction to Hume's Thought." In *The Cambridge Companion to Hume.* Ed. David Fate Norton. Cambridge: Cambridge University Press, 1–32.

Panagia, Davide. 2004. "The Force of Political Argument." *Political Theory* 32 (6): 825–48.

Pasquino, Pasquale. 1998. "Locke on King's Prerogative." *Political Theory* 26 (2): 198– 208.

Pettit, Philip. 2006. *Made with Words: Hobbes on Language, Mind, and Politics.* Princeton, NJ: Princeton University Press.

Pincus, Steve. 2012. "Rethinking Mercantilism: Political Economy, the British Empire, and the Atlantic World in the Seventeenth and Eighteenth Centuries." *William and Mary Quarterly* 69 (1): 3–34.

Pitkin, Hanna. 1967. *The Concept of Representation.* Berkeley: University of California Press.

Pocock, J.G.A. 1975. *The Machiavellian Moment: Florentine Political Thought and the Atlantic Republican Tradition.* Princeton, NJ: Princeton University Press.

———. 1989. "Time, History, and Eschatology in the Thought of Thomas Hobbes." In *Politics, Language, and Time: Essays on Political Thought and History.* Chicago, IL: University of Chicago Press, 148–201.

Poovey, Mary. 1998. *A History of the Modern Fact: Problems of Knowledge in the Sciences of Wealth and Society.* Chicago, IL: University of Chicago Press.

Robin, Corey. 2004. *Fear: The History of a Political Idea.* Oxford: Oxford University Press.

Rogers, G.A.J. 2000. "Hobbes, History and Wisdom." In *Hobbes and History.* Ed. G.A.J. Rogers and Tom Sorrell. London: Routledge, 73–82.

Rothschild, Emma. 2002. *Economic Sentiments: Adam Smith, Condorcet, and the Enlightenment.* Cambridge, MA: Harvard University Press.

———. 2009. "The Atlantic Worlds of David Hume." In *Soundings in Atlantic History: Latent Structures and Intellectual Currents, 1500–1830.* Ed. Bernard Bailyn and Patricia Denault. Cambridge, MA: Harvard University Press, 405–50.

Rothschild, Emma, and Amartya Sen. 2006. "Adam Smith's Economics." In *The Cambridge Companion to Adam Smith.* Ed. Knud Haakonsen. Cambridge: Cambridge University Press, 319–65.

Rotwein, Eugene. 2007. "Introduction." David Hume, *Writings on Economics.* New Brunswick: Transaction Press.

Runciman, David. 2006. *The Politics of Good Intentions: History, Fear, and Hypocrisy in the New World Order.* Princeton, NJ: Princeton University Press.

Sabl, Andrew. 2002. "When Bad Things Happen from Good People (and Vice-Versa): Hume's Political Ethics of Revolution." *Polity* 35 (1): 73–92.

Schaffer, Simon, and Steven Shapin. 1985. *Leviathan and the Air-Pump: Hobbes, Boyle and the Experimental Life*. Princeton, NJ: Princeton University Press.

Schuhmann, Karl. 2000. "Hobbes' Concept of History." In *Hobbes and History*. Ed. G.A.J. Rogers and Tom Sorrell. London: Routledge, 3–24.

Scott, Jonathan. 2000. "The Peace of Silence: Thucydides and the English Civil War." In *Hobbes and History*. Ed. G.A.J. Rogers and Tom Sorrell. London: Routledge, 112–36.

Shapin, Steven. 1994. *A Social History of Truth: Civility and Science in Seventeenth-Century England*. Chicago, IL: University of Chicago Press.

Shapiro, Barbara J. 1983. *Probability and Certainty in Seventeenth-Century England*. Princeton, NJ: Princeton University Press.

Shklar, Judith N. 1998. "The Liberalism of Fear." In *Political Thought and Political Thinkers*. Ed. Stanley Hoffmann. Chicago, IL: University of Chicago Press, 3–20.

Sitter, John. 1982. *Literary Loneliness in Mid-Eighteenth-Century England*. Ithaca, NY: Cornell University Press.

Skinner, Andrew. 1993. "David Hume: Principles of Political Economy." In *The Cambridge Companion to Hume*. Ed. David Fate Norton and Jacqueline Taylor. Cambridge: Cambridge University Press, 381–413.

Smith, Adam. 1981. *An Inquiry into the Nature and Causes of the Wealth of Nations*. Ed. R. H. Campbell and A. S. Skinner. 2 vols. Indianapolis, IN: Liberty Fund.

———. 1982. *Lectures on Jurisprudence*. Ed. R. L. Meek, D. D. Raphael, and P. G. Stein. Indianapolis, IN: Liberty Fund.

———. 2002. *The Theory of Moral Sentiments*. Ed. Knud Haakonsen. Cambridge: Cambridge University Press.

Springborg, Patricia. 2000. "Hobbes and Historiography: Why the Future, He Says, Does Not Exist." In *Hobbes and History*. Ed. G.A.J. Rogers and Tom Sorrell. London: Routledge, 44–72.

Sreedhar, Susanne. 2010. *Hobbes on Resistance: Defying the Leviathan*. Cambridge: Cambridge University Press.

Stern, Philip J. 2012. *The Company State: Corporate Sovereignty and the Early Modern Foundations of the British Empire in India*. Oxford: Oxford University Press.

Stern, Philip J., and Carl Wennerlind. 2013. *Mercantilism Reconsidered: Political Economy in Early Modern Britain and its Empire*. Oxford: Oxford University Press.

Strauss, Leo. 1963. *The Political Philosophy of Hobbes: Its Basis and Its Genesis*. Chicago, IL: University of Chicago Press.

Strong, Tracy B. 1993. "How to Write Scripture: Words, Authority and Politics in Thomas Hobbes." *Critical Inquiry* 20: 128–59.

Tarcov, Nathan. 1981. "Locke's 'Second Treatise' and 'The Best Fence Against Rebellion.'" *Review of Politics* 43 (2): 198–217.

———. 1983. "A 'Non-Lockean' Locke and the Character of Liberalism." In *Liberalism Reconsidered.* Ed. Douglas MacLean and Claudia Mills. Totowa, NJ: Rowman and Allanheld, 130–40.

Tuck, Richard. 1996. "Hobbes' Moral Philosophy." In *The Cambridge Companion to Hobbes.* Ed. Tom Sorrell. Cambridge: Cambridge University Press, 175–207.

———. 2004. "The Utopianism of *Leviathan.*" In Leviathan *After 350 Years.* Ed. Tom Sorrell and Luc Foisneau. Oxford: Oxford University Press, 125–38.

Waldron, Jeremy. 2002. *God, Locke, and Equality: Christian Foundations in Locke's Political Thought.* Cambridge: Cambridge University Press.

Wennerlind, Carl. 2011. *Casualties of Credit: The English Financial Revolution 1620–1720.* Cambridge, MA: Harvard University Press.

Winch, Donald. 1996. *Riches and Poverty: An Intellectual History of Political Economy in Britain, 1750–1834.* Cambridge: Cambridge University Press.

Wolin, Sheldon. 1989. "Democracy and the Welfare State: The Political and Theoretical Connections between *Staatsrason* and *Wohlfahrsstaatsrason.*" In *The Presence of the Past: Essays on the State and the Constitution.* Baltimore, MD: Johns Hopkins University Press, 151–79.

Wood, Neal. 1983. *The Politics of Locke's Philosophy: A Social Study of "An Essay Concerning Human Understanding."* Berkeley: University of California Press.

Wootton, David. 2007. "From Fortune to Feedback: Contingency and the Birth of Modern Political Science." In *Political Contingency: Studying the Unexpected, the Accidental and the Unforeseen.* Ed. Ian Shapiro and Sonu Bedi. New York: New York University Press, 21–53.

Wulf, Steven. 2000. "The Skeptical Life in Hume's Political Thought." *Polity* 33 (1): 77–99.

INDEX

Abizadeh, Arash, 139n29
absolutism/absolutist power, 3, 9–10, 32–35, 38–39; counsel and counselors to, 36–38
accidents, responses to: Hume on, 83; Locke on, 42, 46, 50–51
Adams, John, 135n7
anxiety, 125; Bentham on, 117; Hobbes on, 10, 38; Hume on, 4, 69, 77, 80, 93, 111; Smith on, 106, 120. *See also* fear and fearfulness

Baier, Annette, 139n2
balance of trade: Hume on, 94–95, 110–11; Smith on, 106, 110–12
Beck, Ulrich, 132n7
Bentham, Jeremy, 6, 114–18
Bernstein, Peter, 132n6

Casson, Douglas, 142nn25, 27; 144n37
Christensen, Jerome, 150n26
cloth trade, 92
coinage crises, 45, 64–68
Collins, Jeffrey, 136n17
commerce and trade, 7–8; coinage crises and, 45, 64–68; Hume on, 5, 70, 84, 89–97, 110, 125; Smith on, 5, 96, 100–105, 109, 125–26
common good, 45–47, 51, 53, 57–58
Conniff, James, 150n27
counsel and counselors, 36–38
creditworthiness. *See* trust and credit
Cropsey, Joseph, 152n6

Daston, Lorraine, 147n14, 148nn18–19
Dawson, Hannah, 142n27, 144n37
death, fear of, 29–30

desertion in battle, 139n31
Dienstag, Joshua, 62, 141n12
Douglas, Mary, 154n4
Drucker, Fred, 131n4
Dunn, John, 48, 139n1, 141n13

Elizabeth I, 92
Essex, Earl of, 29
Ewald, François, 1
experiential knowledge: Hobbes on, 10–11, 16–17, 36–38; Hume on, 70, 71–73, 86; Locke on, 42, 57–58; Smith on, 98

fear and fearfulness, 7; Hobbes on, 10, 29–30; Hume on, 4–5, 80–85, 92–93, 96, 127, 128; Smith on, 148n18. *See also* anxiety
fear of death, 29–30
Feldman, Leonard, 142n22
Foucault, Michel, 124–25, 133n7
Freedgood, Elaine, 131n2, 154n2

gambling, 148n19
Garland, David, 133n10, 146n5
geometric method of knowledge: Hobbes on, 3, 11, 13, 21–33, 39–40; Locke on, 136n16
Giddens, Anthony, 132n7
governmentality, 124, 132n7. *See also* politics and political knowledge
Gower, Barry, 76, 146n11
Griswold, Charles, 154nn18, 20

Hacking, Ian, 131n4, 146n7
Hirschman, Albert, 151n32
historical knowledge: Hobbes on, 13, 17–21; Hume on, 149n23

Hobbes, Thomas, 2; on absolutism/
absolutist power, 9–10, 32–35,
38–39; on desertion, 139n31; on
experiential knowledge, 10–11,
16–17, 36–38; on fearfulness and
anxiety, 10, 29–30, 38; on geometric method of knowledge, 3, 11,
13, 21–33, 39–40; on historical
knowledge, 13, 17–21; on language, 22–23, 25, 27, 30, 32, 36; on
politics and political knowledge,
3, 9–12, 21–40; on probabilistic
reasoning, 10, 15; on prudence,
3, 10–12, 13–17, 31, 35–38; on
rebellion and revolution, 139n31,
142n27; "risk," use of, by, 134n2;
on threats to security, 9–12; on
uncertainty, 3, 38, 40, 126, 128
Hont, Istvan, 153n11
hope: Bentham on, 117–18; Hume
on, 5, 70, 80–85, 96–97, 129,
153n7; Smith on, 102, 114–15
Hume, David, 2; on balance of trade,
94–95, 110–11; on commerce and
trade, 5, 70, 84, 89–97, 110, 125;
on experiential knowledge, 70, 71–
73, 86; on fearfulness and anxiety,
4–5, 69, 77, 80–85, 92–93, 96, 111,
127, 128; on historical knowledge,
149n23; on hope, 5, 70, 80–85,
96–97, 129, 153n7; language, use
of, by, 70, 84–85, 89; on mercantilism, 70, 90–91, 94; on politics
and political knowledge, 87–89; on
probabilistic reasoning, 12, 70–80,
81–82, 93, 96, 128; on trust and
credit, 97, 129; on uncertainty, 4,
40, 69, 128

insurance industry, 8, 131n2, 148n19
interest rates, 114–18, 144n36

joint stock companies, 105–9, 151n31

Kahn, Victoria, 138n24
Kleinerman, Benjamin, 141n22

Knight, Frank, 128, 133n11
knowledge: experiential, 10–11,
16–17, 36–38, 42, 57–58, 70–73,
86, 98; geometric, 3, 11, 13, 21–33,
39–40, 136n16; historical, 13,
17–21, 149n23; probabilistic reasoning, 2, 4, 10, 12, 15, 42, 44, 55,
58, 61–62, 70–82, 93, 96, 98, 102,
126–28, 146n6; prudential, 3, 5–6,
10–17, 31, 35–38, 42, 99, 103–4,
118–22, 125, 126; reason/reason-
ing, 143n31; sensory, 44, 56–58

language, uses of: Hobbes and, 22–23,
25, 27, 30, 32, 36; Hume and, 70,
84–85, 89
Laslett, Peter, 48
legislative bodies, 46, 50–51, 58–59
Levy, Jonathan, 131nn2, 3
liberalism, 124–26
Livingston, Donald, 146n4
Locke, John, 2; on accidents, 42, 46,
50–51; on coinage crisis, 45, 64–68;
on the common good, 45–47, 51,
53, 57–58; on experiential knowledge, 42, 57–58; on geometric
method of knowledge, 136n16; on
interest rates, 144n36; on legislative bodies, 46, 50–51, 58–59; on
politics and political knowledge,
4, 43–44, 47–49, 129; on prerogative power, 4, 43, 48–53, 63; on
probabilistic reasoning, 4, 12, 42,
44, 55, 58, 61–62, 128, 146n6; on
prudence, 42; on rebellion and
revolution, 43–44, 48–49, 52,
53–64; on sensory knowledge,
44, 56–58; on trust and credit, 4,
41–44, 47–49, 63, 129; on uncertainty, 4, 40, 42–43, 128
Luhmann, Niklas, 131n2, 132n7

Malcolm, Noel, 136n14
"man of system," 122–23
Mathiowetz, Dean, 136n15
Mehta, Pratap Bhanu, 154n19

mercantilism: Hume on, 70, 90–91, 94; Smith on, 5, 106, 113, 121, 123, 125, 129

modesty, 122–23

monopolies, 106, 112, 153n12

Muldrew, Craig, 135n13, 145n39

Muthu, Sankar, 153n9

Pettit, Philip, 137n19

Pocock, J.G.A, 134n4

politics and political knowledge: Hobbes on, 3, 9–12, 21–40; Hume on, 87–89; Locke on, 4, 43–44, 47–49, 129; Smith on, 105, 109–14, 129

Poovey, Mary, 146n3, 150nn25, 29

prerogative power, 4, 43, 48–53, 63

probabilistic reasoning, 2, 126–28; Hobbes on, 10, 15; Hume on, 12, 70–82, 93, 96, 128; Locke on, 4, 12, 42, 44, 55, 58, 61, 128, 146n6; Smith on, 12, 98, 102

profits and losses. *See* commerce and trade

prudence, 126; Hobbes on, 3, 10–12, 13–17, 31, 35–38; Locke on, 42; Smith on, 5–6, 99, 103–4, 118–22, 125

reason/reasoning, 22, 23, 31, 143n31

rebellion and revolution: Hobbes on, 139n31, 142n27; Locke on, 43–44, 48–49, 52, 53–64

"risk," etymology and use of, 1–2, 127, 154n4; Hobbes and, 134n2; Smith and, 98, 131n3

Rothschild, Emma, 150n24, 152n2

Runciman, David, 133n9

Sen, Amartya, 152n2

sensory knowledge, 44, 56–58

Smith, Adam, 2, 5–6; on balance of trade, 106, 110–12; on coin debasement, 145n40; on commerce and trade, 5, 96, 100–105, 109, 125–26; on fearfulness and anxiety, 106, 120, 148n18; on hope, 102, 114–15; on interest rates, 114–18; on joint stock companies, 105–9, 151n31; on "man of system," 122–23; on mercantilism, 5, 106, 113, 121, 123, 125, 129; on monopolies, 106, 112, 153n12; on politics and political knowledge, 105, 109–14, 129; on probabilistic reasoning, 12, 98, 102; on prudence, 5–6, 99, 103–4, 118–22, 125; "risk," use of, by, 98, 131n3; on trust and credit, 5–6, 100–101, 103–4, 107, 122, 129; on uncertainty, 40, 98–100

sovereign power. *See* absolutism/ absolutist power

subjects (the community/polity): assent to governance by, 35, 39; judgment/decision-making of, 4, 12, 41, 57–62, 64; rights of, 139n31

Thucydides, 18–20

trade. *See* commerce and trade

trust and credit, 7; Hume on, 97, 129; Locke on, 4, 41–44, 47–49, 63, 129; Smith on, 5–6, 100–101, 103–4, 107, 122, 129

Tuck, Richard, 138nn24, 27

uncertainty, 6–7; Hobbes on, 3, 38, 40, 126, 128; Hume on, 4, 40, 69, 128; Locke on, 4, 40, 42–43, 128; Smith on, 40, 98–100

unforeseen events. *See* accidents, responses to

usury. *See* interest rates

visible knowledge. *See* sensory knowledge

Wennerlind, Carl, 144n38

Wootton, David, 148n17

Wulf, Steven, 150n25